Festive Air Fryer Cookbook
© 2024 Future Publishing Limited

Future Books is an imprint of Future PLC
Quay House, The Ambury, Bath, BA1 1UA

A catalogue record for this book is available
from the British Library.

ISBN 978-1-80521-691-9 hardback

The paper holds full FSC certification
and accreditation.

Printed in China by C&C Offset Printing Co. Ltd.
for Future PLC

Interested in Foreign Rights to publish this title?
Email: **licensing@futurenet.com**

Editors
Zara Gaspar and Jane Curran

Deputy Food Editor
Rose Fooks

Art Editor
Lora Barnes

Head of Art & Design
Greg Whitaker

Editorial Director
Jon White

Managing Director
Grainne McKenna

Production Project Manager
Matthew Eglinton

Global Business Development Manager
Jennifer Smith

Senior International Trade Marketing Associate
Kate Waldock

Head of Future International & Bookazines
Tim Mathers

Cover Images
Hannah Hughes, FUTURECONTENTHUB.COM

Images
All copyrights and trademarks are recognised
and respected

FUTURE Connectors.
Creators.
Experience
Makers.

Future plc is a public
company quoted on the
London Stock Exchange
(symbol: FUTR)
www.futureplc.com

Chief Executive Officer **Jon Steinberg**
Non-Executive Chairman **Richard Huntingford**
Chief Financial and Strategy Officer **Penny Ladkin-Brand**

Tel +44 (0)1225 442 244

WELCOME TO

woman&home

The Festive
AIR FRYER
COOKBOOK

We all love our air fryers, and this book is here to help it work for you over the busy holiday season. Nobody would claim you can cook a whole Christmas lunch in an air fryer, but you can still use it in so many ways.

First of all, it works as an extension to your main oven — after all, it's a mini oven in its own right. Veggies can be reheated to delightfully crisp, a vegetarian or vegan dish can be cooked separately away from the main course meat, or a stunning starter soufflé can be doing its thing while the turkey is roasting away. When it comes to party food, it's a winner. We are big fans of making sausage rolls, cheesy pastries and spring rolls in a large batch, then open-freezing them before bagging them up into freezer bags (don't forget to label …). Then you can bake them speedily in the air fryer as needed when friends and family arrive. And yes, you can feel a little smug at this point — no slaving around a hot oven in your party clothes on New Year's Eve. Check out our fab recipes on page 16. For those days in between, there's the best pork belly ever and delicious soups made from roasted, seasonal vegetables. And an air fryer is perfect for reheating leftovers. Our sweet-toothed friends haven't been left out, with new ideas for a cheesecake, different bakes and yes — you can bake a Christmas cake in an air fryer in less time than a conventional oven, so why not get ahead and be prepared for the holidays. We've plenty of tips and tricks to help, whether you're new to air fryers or a seasoned pro.

So save time, save a bit of money on those dreaded energy bills and make your air fryer work for you over the festive season.

PARTY FOOD

41

17

32

STARTERS

66

67

New to Air Frying? See page 10 for tips on what to cook and how.

MAINS

74

90

76

DESSERTS & BAKES

IN-BETWEEN

KNOW YOUR
AIR FRYER

**New to air frying? Here's some tips on how it works,
what cooks well in it, and importantly, what doesn't**

WHAT IS AN AIR FRYER?

It's basically a small convection oven with a built-in fan. By circulating really hot air around your food at high speed, an air fryer will cook your food using a fraction of the oil you'd normally use for deep frying. So not only is it quicker than cooking food in your oven, cutting down on your energy use, it's healthier too. As it's a mini oven, you can reheat food easily and sometimes, it works better than a microwave for reheating foods where you want to get a crisp texture back, such as pizza, slices of quiche, roast potatoes and chicken nuggets. Of course you can cook from scratch, though some foods work better than others and are easier to cook on a hob. It's a good friend to have for the holidays, too, when you may want to free up space in your main oven or want to cook a few sausage rolls when friends turn up. The many air fryers on the market differ, with various pre-set functions, single or dual baskets and of course with different capacities, depending how you think you'll use it and how many you are cooking for. It also heats to temperature in around three minutes, far quicker than a conventional oven.

"The trick with homemade chips is to soak them in cold water for about 15 minutes before air frying"

WHICH RECIPES WORK BEST?

Chips, of course, but you already knew that! The trick with homemade chips is to soak them in cold water for about 15 minutes before air frying. This draws out the starch for a crisp result. Dry them well before frying. Anything which has a crumb, such as schnitzels, fish fingers and nuggets, are crisp and crunchy without all that oil, with far less mess and kitchen smells. Ditto battered fish from the freezer. Use it for roasting vegetables and for roasting small joints of meat. It cooks pork belly brilliantly (see our recipe on page 75), giving the best crackling ever. Even roast potatoes are cooked in no time. Be aware, though, that crowding food will just give a soggy result, so your roasties need to have a bit of space between them, in a single layer. Bacon crisps up without the need to add extra fat and making cleaning much quicker. Sausages are also a good bet. And crispy Chinese-style duck? You can really give the takeaway a miss here with our recipe on page 159. Bakers are not forgotten, either. Cookies, cupcakes and muffins are ready in a jiffy. Try using it for energy bars and flapjacks.

THE PRACTICAL STUFF

Once you've decided on the best air fryer which works for you, position it on the kitchen countertop so it has space around it – particularly behind it – so that the fan can circulate easily and efficiently. Air fryers are

easy to clean in hot soapy water, but they clean quicker if they aren't left to go stone cold. Using parchment liners, silicone liners or part-lining the basket with foil will make the job easier.

Obviously space in the air fryer basket is restricted, unlike a conventional oven. So you may need to buy extra kit, such as smaller cake and baking tins, gratin dishes and ramekins. We are big fans of individual silicone muffin and cupcake cases which don't need oiling before using. Some machines come with a kitchen thermometer probe, which really helps when cooking meat and poultry. If yours doesn't, then invest in one for all your kitchen needs – beef will never be overcooked again. Kebabs cook quickly in an air fryer, so some metal skewers which fit are handy. An oil spray will get plenty of use.

PARTY FOOD

BUFFET OR CANAPÉS, YOUR GET-TOGETHER WILL GO OFF WITHOUT A HITCH

Smoky Parmesan Melts

Delicious crumbly, savoury shortbread, perfect with a pre-dinner drink. The recipe makes a large amount, so we recommend open-freezing them raw, bagging them up, then air fry from frozen as you need them

Makes around 50 * Ready in 15 minutes, plus freezing

- 125g (4½oz) plain flour, plus extra for dusting
- ¼tsp baking powder
- ¼tsp smoked paprika
- Pinch cayenne pepper
- 100g (3½oz) unsalted butter, diced
- 60g (2½oz) Gruyère, grated
- 60g (2½oz) Parmesan cheese
- 1 small egg, beaten
- 1tbsp pine nuts, optional

1 Line 2 baking trays with baking paper. Put the flour, baking powder, paprika and cayenne pepper in a food processor. Add the butter and pulse until the mixture resembles fine crumbs. Then add the cheeses and continue to blend until the dough just comes together.

2 Turn out the dough onto a big sheet of baking parchment. Roll, with the help of the paper, into a long cylinder, around 30cm (12in) long and 4cm (1½in) circumference. Chill for 15 mins, then cut 2mm (⅛in) circles, placing them on the lined trays. Brush each cookie with a little beaten egg and push a pine nut in the centre. Open freeze, then put into labelled freezer bags when frozen.

3 To cook, heat the air fryer to 170°C/325°F. Bake the biscuits on a silicone liner for 5 mins, then flip and bake for 2 mins.

> **"Delicious crumbly, savoury shortbread, perfect with a pre-dinner drink"**

Olive Straws

We've given these easy cheesy straws an inviting olive twist! These are best open-frozen when raw, bagged up for the freezer, then air fried when you want them

Makes around 20 • **Ready in 25 minutes**

- 500g (1lb 2oz) all butter puff pastry
- 5tbsp black olive tapenade
- 2tbsp grated Parmesan
- 1 egg, beaten
- 1tsp picked thyme leaves

You will need:
1 baking tray, lined

1 Roll the puff pastry out to a large rectangle approximately 30 x 40cm (12 x 16in).
2 With the pastry as landscape, spread the tapenade over the bottom half. Scatter over most of the cheese, reserving some for the top. Then fold the naked side over, glaze with the beaten egg and sprinkle the remaining cheese and thyme leaves on top. Push gently with your hands to flatten down the cheese.

3 Trim the sides to create a nice sharp edge. Then cut into 20 x 1½cm (just under ¾in) thick strips. As you pick up each piece, stretch it and twist it a few times, then place onto the baking tray. Press down the ends to stop them unravelling. Open freeze then bag up for the freeze until you are ready to bake.
4 Heat the air fryer to 200°C/400°F. Bake the olive straws for 5 mins, turning them halfway through.

17

Lamb Meatball Lettuce Cups

A refreshing canapé choice for guests looking for a less filling, healthier option

**Makes around 20-25 *
Ready in 20 minutes**

* * 1 small red onion, finely sliced
* * 2tbsp red wine vinegar
* * 20 lamb meatballs (around 500g/1lb 2oz)
* * 2 little gem lettuces
* * 100g (3½oz) feta, crumbled
* * 6tbsp strained Greek yoghurt
* * 3tbsp freshly chopped mint
* * Pomegranate seeds, to garnish
* * 2tsp za'atar (or use a mix of sesame seeds and dried herbs)
* * 2tbsp olive oil

1 Heat the air fryer to 180°C/350°F. Toss the red onion in the vinegar and set aside, stirring occasionally.
2 Air fry the meatballs for 14 mins, turning halfway.
3 Meanwhile, give the lettuce a thorough wash, break into leaves and arrange on a platter.
4 Mix the feta, yoghurt and mint, and grind over some black pepper.
5 Break the meatballs in 2 and arrange 1-2 pieces on each lettuce leaf. Top each with a couple of teaspoons of yoghurt mixture, some slices of onion and the pomegranate seeds. Mix the za'atar and oil, and drizzle over them.

Baba Ghanoush

This moreish Middle Eastern dip is made in an air fryer in less than half the time of a conventional oven

Serves around 10 * **Ready in 30 minutes**

* 3 medium aubergines
* Olive oil spray
* 2 garlic cloves
* 2½tbsp tahini paste
* 1tsp cumin seeds, toasted

* **3tbsp lemon juice (approx 1 lemon)**
* **Handful of fresh parsley, chopped**
* **Pomegranate seeds, optional**

1 Heat the air fryer to 200°C/400°F. Cut the aubergines in half lengthways, and score the flesh in a criss-cross pattern, being careful not to cut through the skin. Spray the aubergine halves with the oil, put into the air fryer skin side down (you may need to do this in 2 batches), and air fry for 20 mins until the flesh is soft.

2 Remove from the air fryer and leave to cool. Place the garlic, tahini, cumin, remaining olive oil, aubergine flesh (discard the skins) and lemon juice into a food processor and blitz until it reaches a dip consistency.

3 Season to taste and scatter with parsley and the pomegranate seeds.

"Serve this smoky aubergine dip with flatbread or crackers"

Cook's tip
If you can't find pre-cooked ham hock, shred or chop some smoked ham instead.

Mini Croque Monsieur Swirls

Buttery pastry, smoky ham and melted cheese – what's not to resist?

Makes around 30 * Ready in 30 minutes, plus freezing time

* 15g (½oz) butter, melted
* 1tbsp plain flour, plus extra for dusting
* 125ml (4fl oz) whole milk
* 1tsp English mustard powder
* 1tbsp lemon thyme leaves
* 325g (11oz) ready-rolled puff pastry
* 100g (3½oz) cooked ham hock
* 45g (1½oz) Emmental cheese, grated

1 Make a béchamel sauce: mix the butter and flour in a pan on a gentle heat until smooth. Add the milk, a little at a time, while whisking away any lumps. Cook until thick, remove from the heat and stir in the mustard, thyme and a grind of pepper. Leave to cool, the surface covered with cling film.

2 Unroll the pastry and dust the underneath with flour. Turn sideways and cut in half – you'll have two 15 x 24cm (6 x 9½in) pieces. Spread the béchamel equally over both pieces of pastry. Scatter over the ham and cheese, and season with pepper.

3 Roll the pastry up the long ways to make two 24cm (9½in) long rolls. Chill for at least 15 mins until firm, or if making ahead, the rolls can be left in the fridge for a day.

4 Cut into 2cm (¾in) thick slices. Open freeze on parchment-lined trays, then bag up once frozen.

5 To bake, heat the air fryer to 200°C/400°F. Bake the pastries for 6 mins, then turn and bake for a further 2-3 mins until browned.

Halloumi Chips

These are usually deep-fried, but cooked in an air fryer, the result is just as melting, crisp and delicious

Makes around 40 • **Ready in 30 minutes**

- **2 x 225g (8oz) blocks halloumi**
- **3tbsp plain flour**
- **1tbsp smoked paprika**
- **1tbsp chilli powder**
- **2 eggs, beaten**
- **120g (4oz) panko breadcrumbs**
- **Oil spray**
- **Dips to serve, such as sriracha mayonnaise**

1 Slice your blocks of halloumi into sticks, each one roughly the size of a thick finger. Combine the flour, paprika and chilli and place on a plate. Pour the egg into a shallow dish, and scatter the breadcrumbs onto a final plate. Coat the halloumi sticks with the flour mixture, then the egg and finally the panko. Heat the air fryer to 180°C/350°F. Spray the sticks with oil. Air fry the sticks in batches for 8 mins, turning halfway through.

"The perfect, cheesy treat for a party snack"

Crustless Smoked Salmon Tartlets

Unless you have metal mini cupcake tins which fit your air fryer, we find that individual silicone cupcake cases do the job perfectly. Cook in two batches

Makes 12 • Ready in 15 minutes

• 3 eggs
• 100g (3½oz) crème fraîche, plus 2tbsp for serving
• 100g (3½oz) smoked salmon, shredded
• 1 small cooked beetroot (not pickled), approx 30g (1oz), chopped into small dice
• 1tbsp dill, finely chopped, plus a few extra sprigs for serving

You will need:
6 individual silicone cupcake cases

1 In a large jug, beat the eggs and mix in the crème fraîche until nicely combined. Season with a little salt and plenty of black pepper.

2 Divide half the smoked salmon, beetroot and chopped dill between the cupcake cases. Heat the air fryer to 160°C/300°F. Put the cases on a flat tin and pour over the egg mixture until the filling is just covered.

3 Bake for 8 mins until firm with just a slight wobble. Leave to cool slightly before carefully releasing each tartlet. Repeat with the remaining mixture.

4 Place a small spoonful of crème fraîche and a sprig of dill on top of each tartlet before serving. These are best served warm.

Spiced Paneer and Pickled Red Onion Poppadom Cups

Mini poppadoms with tangy onion, spiced cheese and a creamy coriander yoghurt

Makes 26 * Ready in 20 minutes, plus marinating

* 1tsp fresh ginger, peeled and grated
* ½tsp grated garlic
* Juice of 1 lime, plus wedges to serve
* 3tbsp Greek yoghurt
* ¼tsp chilli flakes
* ½tsp ground cumin
* ½tsp garam masala
* ¼tsp nigella seeds
* 8tsp turmeric
* 225g (8oz) paneer, cut into 2 x 2cm (¾ x ¾in) cubes
* 1 red onion, thinly sliced
* 1tbsp red wine vinegar
* 1tbsp sugar
* 4tbsp natural yoghurt
* 1tbsp fresh coriander, plus extra to serve
* 26 mini poppadoms

1 Combine the ginger, garlic, lime juice, Greek yoghurt and spices. Add the cubes of paneer and coat in the marinade. This can be done the night before, but leave to marinate for at least 15 mins.
2 In a bowl, mix the red onion with the vinegar and sugar. Scrunch together with your hands and you'll feel the sugar start to dissolve. Rest for at least 10 mins.
3 In a food processor, blitz the natural yoghurt and coriander together. Add 1tbsp water to loosen the mixture. Set aside.
4 Heat the air fryer to 200°C/400°F. Bake the paneer on a silicone or parchment liner for 7 mins.
5 Pile a little red onion mix into each poppadom, then top with the hot paneer and drizzle with coriander yoghurt and a sprinkle of chopped coriander. Serve immediately, with lime wedges.

Prawn Cocktail Lettuce Cups

An easy party nibble, bring back the retro favourite, prawn cocktail

Makes around 12 * Ready in 15 minutes

* 1 red onion, thinly sliced
* 2tbsp white wine vinegar
* 1tsp caster sugar
* 300g (10oz) raw, peeled king prawns
* Olive oil spray
* 5tbsp thick yoghurt
* 2tbsp crème fraîche
* 3tbsp tomato ketchup
* 2tsp Dijon mustard
* 1 baby gem, leaves separated
* Small bunch parsley, finely chopped
* Smoked paprika, to garnish

1 Put the onion, vinegar and sugar in a small bowl, mix and set aside to pickle. Heat the air fryer to 180°C/350°F. Spray the prawns with oil and air fry for 5 mins, shaking the basket halfway through. Set aside to cool.
2 Mix the yoghurt, crème fraîche, ketchup and mustard together. Add the prawns and coat in the sauce.
3 Just before serving, spoon a heaped tablespoon of prawn mixture into each lettuce leaf. Top with the pickled onions, parsley and a pinch of smoked paprika.

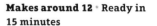

"Host a fondue party for the ultimate winter warmer crowd-pleaser"

Fondue with Mini Roasties

Is there anything better than a crispy roast potato? Yes – the addition of melted cheese!

Serves 6-8 * Ready in 30 minutes

* 750g (1lb 11oz) baby new potatoes
* 2tbsp olive oil
* 3 sprigs of thyme
* 100g (3½oz) Comté, grated
* 100g (3½oz) Gruyère, grated
* 100g (3½oz) Emmental, grated
* 2tsp cornflour
* 1 garlic clove
* 350ml (12fl oz) dry white wine, small glass of Calvados or kirsch

1 Heat the air fryer to 200°C/400°F. Toss the potatoes in the oil with plenty of sea salt. Put the thyme into the air fryer, then add the potatoes. Cook for 20 mins, giving them a shake halfway through.
2 Meanwhile, mix together the cheese and cornflour. Rub the base of a pan with the garlic then discard. Add the wine to the pan and heat until simmering gently. The trick is to add the cheese gradually, stirring all the time – like making risotto.
3 As the cheese melts, add another handful. Once all the cheese has been incorporated and the mixture has thickened, stir in the Calvados. Serve as a dip with the potatoes.

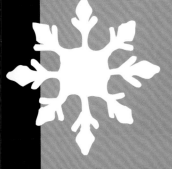

Goat's Cheese and Fig Stars

Lightly melted cheese with sweet figs and honey ready in minutes

You will need:
* Star biscuit cutter

Makes 20 * Ready in 20 minutes

* 325g (11oz) all butter ready-rolled puff pastry
* 1 egg, beaten
* 1 small log goat's cheese, cut into 20 half-moon shapes
* 4 figs, each one cut into 5 wedges
* A generous drizzle of honey
* ½tsp sumac

1 Heat the air fryer to 190°C/375°F. Cut out star shapes from the sheet of puff pastry and place on a baking tray. Brush each shape with egg wash. Top with a piece of goat's cheese and a fig wedge.
2 Air fry in batches for 5 mins on a silicone or parchment mat. Drizzle with honey and sprinkle over the sumac. Allow to cool slightly before serving.

Goat's Cheese and Cranberry Tartlets

These are quick and easy to make, and stay hot for some time. The crunchy, buttery cases will suit all sorts of fillings. You'll need to bake them in two batches for the air fryer

Makes 12 • Ready in 15 minutes

• **12 slices of thick white sandwich bread**
• **60g (2oz) butter, softened**
• **12tbsp relish or chutney**
• **200g (7oz) goat's cheese**
• **Snipped chives, to serve**

You will need:
7½cm (3in) round cutter, and silicone cupcake cases

1 Cut a disc from each slice of bread, butter and place butter-side down into the cases. Heat the air fryer to 200°C/400°F.
2 Spoon 2tsp of relish into each tartlet – it should reach almost to the top of the bread. Place a slice of cheese on top. Press the cheese into the relish. Bake for 10 mins until the cheese has begun to melt and has browned a little. Sprinkle with chives.

Garlic Ginger Pork Belly Skewers

Crisp on the outside and tender on the inside, these make a delicious starter

Makes around 20 * Ready in 30 minutes, plus overnight marinating

* **850g (1lb 14oz) skinless thick pork belly slices, cut into bite-sized chunks**
* **3tbsp sesame oil**
* **7tbsp Japanese soy sauce**
* **4cm (1½in) piece ginger, peeled and grated**
* **2 garlic cloves, grated**
* **2tbsp dark brown sugar**
* **2tbsp rice wine vinegar**
* **1 courgette, peeled into strips**
* **1 carrot, cut lengthways into strips**

1 Put the pork belly in a large dish. Mix the sesame oil with 2 tablespoons of the soy sauce, the ginger and garlic and pour this over the pork. Toss to coat well, cover and marinate in the fridge for a minimum of 2 hrs, preferably overnight.

2 To make the glaze add the remaining soy sauce to a saucepan with the sugar and rice vinegar. Bring to the boil, reduce the heat and simmer until syrupy. Heat the air fryer to 200°C/400°F.

3 Place the pork in the air fryer and cook for 5 mins. Flip over and cook for 3 mins. Brush over the glaze and cook for a further 2 mins.

4 Thread a ribbon of courgette or carrot onto a cocktail stick and then add a cube of pork.

Cook's tip
If you have leftover glaze, serve it on the side as a dip.

Baked Camembert Fondue Loaf

You'll need to buy a round country-style loaf which fits your air fryer, usually no bigger than 20cm (8in) at its largest width

Serves 6 · **Ready in 40 minutes**

- 1 boule bread loaf (we used sourdough)
- Olive oil spray
- 1 ripe Camembert, around 400g (14oz)
- 2tbsp white wine
- 1 sprig rosemary, leaves finely chopped
- A little honey, for drizzling, optional

1 Slice off the top of the loaf, then cut a hole in the bread just big enough for the Camembert to sit in. Cut the off-cut bread into croutons for dipping. Heat the air fryer to 200°C/400°F. Spray the bread and toss in the oil. Air fry for 5 mins, shaking halfway through, then set aside. Reduce the temperature to 180°C/350°F.

2 Put the Camembert into the hole and score the top in a diamond shape.

3 Drizzle the wine over the cheese, place the bread in the air fryer and bake for 25 mins, then reduce to 140°C/250°F, sprinkle over the rosemary and bake for a further 10 mins. Leave in for a few mins. Drizzle over the honey if using.

4 Serve the cheese hot with the croutons and any extra sides you like.

Cook's tip

The Camembert must be ripe and at room temperature for the best, and fastest result. Serve with a selection of charcuterie and pickles on the side.

Glazed Leek, Apple and Sausage Skewers

It's worth investing in metal skewers which fit in your air fryer, as it's so good for any kebab-style dishes

Makes 15 • Ready in 20 minutes

- **30 mini chipolata sausages**
- **1 small leek, cleaned, halved lengthwise and cut into 4cm (1½in) chunks**
- **2 tart eating apples, cut into 4cm (1½in) chunks**
- **Olive oil spray**

FOR THE GLAZE:
- **2tbsp runny honey**
- **1tbsp wholegrain mustard**
- **1tsp olive oil**
- **2 sprigs thyme, leaves picked**

You will also need:
15 x 11cm (6 x 4½in) skewers

1 Heat the air fryer to 200°C/400°F. Thread two sausages and a piece each of leek and apple onto each skewer. Spray with oil and air fry for 10 mins.

2 Meanwhile, for the glaze, combine the honey, mustard and olive oil. Drizzle over the sausages and air fry for a further 3 mins.

3 Remove from the air fryer and garnish skewers with thyme leaves. Serve on a platter with a dipping bowl of ketchup or a spicy sauce, if liked.

Cheesy Olive Bites

Perfect to serve with drinks, these take a bit of effort to prepare, but are air fried in minutes

Makes 50 • Ready in 1 hour

- 100g (3½oz) unsalted butter, softened
- 100g (3½oz) Cheddar cheese, finely grated
- 150g (5oz) plain flour
- ¼tsp cayenne pepper
- 1 egg, beaten
- 3 dashes Worcestershire sauce
- 50 (about 150g/5oz) pimento stuffed olives (pitted)
- Oil spray

1 Beat the butter until creamy in a large mixing bowl, add the cheese and mix well. Stir in the flour, cayenne pepper and a pinch of sea salt.
2 Beat the egg with 2tbsp cold water and the Worcestershire sauce. Add to the dough and mix just until incorporated. Refrigerate for 30 mins.
3 Remove the olives from the jar and dry with kitchen paper. Tear off an olive-sized piece of dough, press into a disc, place an olive onto the disc and shape the dough around it, pinching to repair breaks. Place onto a baking tray. Repeat the process with the remaining dough and olives.
4 Heat the air fryer to 200°C/400°F. Spray the bites with oil, then air fry in 3 batches for 8 mins, giving them a shake in the basket after 5 mins.

35

Spiced Maple Nut Mix

Offering the perfect balance of sweet and salty, this also provides a delicious kick of spice for good measure. It's ideal when served with a glass of fizz or your favourite festive cocktail, and also makes a wonderful edible gift

Serves 12 * **Ready in 20 minutes**

* 400g (14oz) natural (raw) mixed nuts
* 4tbsp maple syrup
* 2tsp mixed spice
* 2tsp sweet paprika
* 100g (3½oz) mixed cranberries and chopped apricot pieces

1 Heat the air fryer to 180°C/350°F. Put the nuts in a large bowl, and mix in the maple syrup, spices and 1tsp sea salt.
2 Air fry on liners for 7 mins in two batches, stirring halfway through. Allow to cool. Finally, mix through the dried fruits.

Cook's tip
Make sure the mix is cool before sealing jars to keep its crunch.

Asian Sausage Rolls

These have an added zing of spice and take just minutes to air fry

Makes 20 * **Ready in 35 minutes**

* 400g (14oz) minced pork
* 3tbsp kecap manis (sweet soy sauce)
* 1tbsp sesame oil
* 4 spring onions, finely sliced (including the green part)
* ¼tsp Chinese five spice
* ½tsp dried chilli flakes
* 375g (13oz) puff pastry
* 1 egg, beaten
* 2tbsp sesame seeds

1 Mix the mince with the kecap manis, sesame oil, spring onions, five spice and chilli flakes, and season well.

2 Roll out the pastry to 30 x 50cm (12 x 19½in). Cut lengthwise in half. Spread the meat down each length, and brush one side with egg. Fold over the opposite side of the pastry and use a fork to seal. Trim the edge. Brush with egg and sprinkle over sesame seeds. Cut into 3cm-long (1¼in-long) rolls.

3 Heat the air fryer to 200°C/ 400°F. Bake in batches for 8 mins. If baking from frozen, add 2-3 extra mins to the cooking time, checking they are cooked through and piping hot before serving.

"A modern take on the star of any festive buffet table"

Miso Prawn Skewers

We've left these prawns with heads on here, but you can cut the heads off when peeling

Makes around 12 * Ready in 10 minutes, plus marinating

* 12 raw tiger prawns, peeled but heads left intact
* Juice of ½ lemon
* 3tbsp white miso paste
* Olive oil spray
* Lime wedges and chopped spring onions or chives, to serve

You will need:
Small skewers

1 Mix the prawns with the lemon juice and miso paste, and refrigerate for 30 mins, to marinate.
2 Heat the air fryer to 200°C/400°F. Skewer each prawn, spray with oil and cook for 5 mins, flipping halfway through. Serve with lime wedges, and spring onions or chives, if you like.

Gorgonzola Gougères

If you're throwing a fun soirée this festive season, then make sure you have some of these on the table – they are always a total crowd-pleaser! Again, it's a large amount and it's too fiddly to pipe into an air fryer, so open freeze then bag them up until you're ready to bake

Makes around 60 • Ready in 30 minutes, plus freezing

FOR THE HERBY CRUMBLE:
* 4tbsp plain flour
* 15g (½oz) butter, cold
* 50g (2oz) hard blue cheese
* 2tbsp walnuts, chopped
* ½ small bunch herbs, such as parsley or tarragon, leaves picked

FOR THE CHOUX PASTRY:
* 90g (3oz) butter
* 150ml (5fl oz) dry white wine
* 180g (6¼oz) plain flour
* 6 eggs, beaten
* 150g (5oz) Gorgonzola, mashed to a paste
* Chutney, to serve

You will need:
2 baking trays, lined, and a piping bag

1 For the herby crumble, pulse the ingredients in a food processor until they've formed a crumble. Decant into a bowl and chill until required.
2 For the choux pastry, melt the butter with the wine and 150ml (5fl oz) water. Bring to the boil and remove from the heat. Add the flour in one go and mix vigorously into a smooth paste until the ball of dough comes away from the sides. Then place in a bowl, spreading the paste up the sides to cool quicker.
3 Once cooled, add in the eggs, one at a time, using an electric hand whisk. Add in the Gorgonzola and whisk until smooth.
4 Transfer the mix to a piping bag, cut the end and pipe small bulbs on both trays. Sprinkle with the herby crumble then open-freeze and bag up.
5 To bake, heat the air fryer to 200°C/400°F. Bake the choux buns in batches on an air fryer liner for 8 mins. Serve piping hot with your favourite chutney, if you like.

Classic Salmon Blinis

These always go down well. We've jazzed up the cream cheese and swapped the smoked salmon for something a little bit different. If you want to make these vegetarian, omit the salmon and serve them with a spoonful of your favourite chutney

Makes 24 * **Ready in 15 minutes**

* 150g (5oz) piece salmon fillet
* Olive oil spray
* 250g (9oz) cream cheese
* 1tbsp horseradish cream
* 1tbsp capers, finely chopped
* ½ large shallot, finely chopped
* 5-6 cornichons (mini gherkins), finely chopped
* Juice of ½ lemon
* 24 ready-made blinis
* Dill, to garnish

1 Heat the air fryer to 180°C/375°F. Spray the salmon with a little oil and season. Bake on an air fryer liner for 8 mins. Set aside to cool. Mix the cream cheese, horseradish, capers, shallot, cornichons and lemon juice together, and season with salt and pepper.
2 Arrange the blinis on a platter and add a spoonful of the cream cheese mix to each one. Flake over the salmon and then garnish with the fresh dill.

> "These bite-sized delights are a twist on the classic canapé"

STARTERS

GET DINNER OFF TO A DELICIOUS START
WITH THESE FESTIVE APPETISERS

Pear with Ginger and Walnuts

Firm but not rock-hard pears are best for cooking. This is a quick, simple starter, light enough to serve before a big meal

Serves 4 * Ready in 25 minutes

* 4 firm pears
* 3tbsp soft brown sugar
* 30g (1oz) butter
* ¼tsp grated nutmeg
* 2 knobs stem ginger in syrup, finely chopped
* 60g (2½oz) walnuts, finely chopped (reserve a few to serve)

* 100g (3½oz) Stilton or other blue cheese

To serve:
* 2 endive or chicory
* Handful rocket
* Balsamic syrup

1 Slice the pears in half, then use a melon baller to scoop out the seeds.
2 Melt the sugar and butter in a small saucepan. Add the pears flat side down and leave for a few mins to caramelise. Heat the air fryer to 180°C/350°F.

3 Put the pears on an air fryer liner and bake for 10 mins. Remove and allow to cool slightly. Scoop a large portion of the pear out of the shell — keeping the main intact. Finely chop the filling and mix this with the nutmeg, stem ginger, walnuts and Stilton.
4 Fill the pears with the nutty filling and return to the air fryer to bake for 5 mins. Remove, and allow to cool slightly before serving with endive, chicory or rocket, a drizzle of balsamic and a few walnut pieces.

Roast Butternut Squash Soup

Roasting the squash in an air fryer makes it much sweeter

Serves 6 * **Ready in 40 minutes**

* **750g (1lb 10oz) butternut squash, deseeded and cubed**
* **1tbsp oil**
* **1 onion, chopped**
* **2tsp ground coriander**
* **2 medium-sized sweet potatoes, cubed**
* **1¾l (3pt) vegetable stock**
* **150ml (5fl oz) soured cream**
* **1tsp crushed pink peppercorns**

1 Heat the air fryer to 180°C/350°F. Toss the squash in the oil and roast in the air fryer for 20 mins, shaking the drawer halfway through. You may need to do this in two batches. Meanwhile, heat the remaining oil in a large pan. Add the onion and fry gently for 5 mins, to soften. Add the ground coriander and cook for 1-2 mins. When the squash is tender, add it to the onions, the sweet potatoes and pour in the vegetable stock. Bring to the boil and simmer for 15 mins, until the vegetables are tender.
2 Pour the soup, in batches, into a blender and whizz until smooth. (You can prepare this a couple of days in advance, and chill in an airtight container or freeze it.)
3 To serve, warm the soup through thoroughly, swirl in the soured cream and add a sprinkling of crushed pink peppercorns.

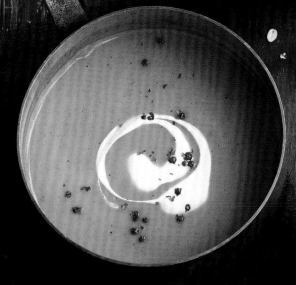

"If you want to add a bit of richness to your soup, scatter some croutons over it"

Med-style Potted Goat's Cheese

A fab alternative to a meat pâté, and the tasty olive toasts are the perfect crunchy addition

Serves 6 * **Ready in 10 minutes, plus chilling**

* 1 loaf olive bread
* 1 clove of garlic, crushed
* 2tbsp extra virgin olive oil

FOR THE POTTED CHEESE:
* 300g (10½oz) soft goat's cheese
* 100g (3½oz) light cream cheese
* A little basil, chopped, plus leaves to garnish
* 50g (2oz) sun-dried tomatoes in oil, drained and chopped
* 50g (2oz) pitted black olives, chopped
* 2tbsp capers, chopped

1 Heat the air fryer to 200°C/400°F. Slice the bread. Mix the garlic with 1tbsp oil and season. Brush a little on the bread and air fry for 1-2 mins a side, or until crisp and golden. Cool and store in an airtight container.
2 For the potted cheese, mix together all the ingredients (reserving a few tomatoes, olives, capers and basil leaves to garnish). Season, spoon into ramekins and chill. To serve, drizzle with the remaining oil and add the garnishes. Serve with the toasts.

> **"Serve as crostini instead of in ramekins for canapés"**

Red Rice and Roots

A deliciously earthy salad, great as a starter or as a dish for a festive buffet

Serves 4 * Ready in 2 hours

* 450g (1lb) raw beetroot
* 150g (5oz) red rice
* Grated zest and juice of 1 orange
* 2tbsp olive oil
* 2tbsp shelled pistachios, roughly chopped
* 100g (3½oz) feta cheese, crumbled
* Good handful of mint leaves, roughly chopped/torn or whole

1 Heat the air fryer to 200°C/400°F. Trim the beetroot, leaving a little bit of stalk on them, then wrap in foil leaving space for air to circulate, but seal well, then air fry for up to 1 hr 30 mins, depending on size, until tender.

2 Meanwhile, add rice to a pan of boiling water and simmer for 30 mins. Drain and cool.

3 While still warm, peel, quarter and slice the beetroot and put in a large bowl with the orange zest and juice, and the oil.

4 Add the rice, pistachios, feta cheese and mint. Season well. Mix in gently.

Roast Veg Medley Pies

These delicious pies are packed with sweet roasted veg. Roast them in batches

Makes 4 * Ready in 1 hour 40 minutes

- 200g (7oz) carrots, peeled and sliced into rounds
- 1tsp caraway seeds
- Olive oil spray
- 150g (5oz) cauliflower, cut into florets
- 2 leeks, sliced into thin rounds
- 200ml (7fl oz) vegetable stock
- 2 garlic cloves, peeled
- 1tbsp thyme leaves
- 3tbsp crème fraîche
- 2tsp English mustard
- 200g (7oz) cooked beetroot, diced
- 2tbsp chopped flat-leaf parsley
- 75g (3oz) Cheddar, grated
- 50g (2oz) Gruyère, grated
- Plain flour, for dusting
- 450g (1lb) puff pastry
- 2 egg yolks, plus 1tbsp milk, lightly beaten, for glazing

1 Heat the air fryer to 180°C/ 350°F. Put the carrots and caraway seeds in a dish, spray with oil then roast for 15 mins. Set aside. Spray the cauliflower with oil, air fry for 12 mins, shaking the draw a few times.
2 Cook the leeks, stock, garlic and thyme in a sauté pan, uncovered, until tender.
3 Retrieve the garlic cloves, and mash to a paste with a fork. Add the leeks to a large bowl with the other veg. Mix the garlic, crème fraîche and mustard in a small bowl, then stir this through the veg. Cool completely, then stir through the parsley and grated cheeses.
4 On a floured surface, roll the pastry out to a 35cm (14in) square. Cut into 4 equal squares. Brush the edges with egg glaze and pile equal amounts of filling into the centre of each. Lift opposite corners over the filling and pinch together. Repeat with the other corners. Now pinch the edges, to seal the pies and put them on a large, lined baking tray. Chill for atleast 30 mins.
5 Heat the air fryer to 180°C/ 350°F. Brush with egg, scatter over some caraway seeds and bake for 20 mins, flipping halfway through, until golden and piping hot.

49

Twice-baked Cheese Soufflé

Prepare a few hours ahead then finish on the big day; a great way to get ahead this Christmas!

Serves 4 * Ready in 30 minutes

* 175ml (6fl oz) milk
* 1 shallot, halved
* ½tsp pink peppercorns
* 30g (1oz) unsalted butter, plus extra for greasing
* 2tbsp plain flour
* 1tsp Dijon mustard
* 125g (4oz) Gruyère cheese, grated
* 2 eggs, separated
* 150ml (5fl oz) double cream
* Watercress, to serve, optional

You will need:
4 x ramekin dishes, around 150ml (5fl oz) capacity, brushed with melted butter

1 Heat the milk with the shallot and peppercorns, but don't boil.
2 Melt the butter in a pan, add the flour and stir to create a roux. Sieve the milk mixture, removing the shallot and peppercorns and gradually whisk this into the roux to make a thick white sauce. Beat in the mustard, 100g (3½oz) cheese and the egg yolks, then season. Heat the air fryer to 200°C/400°F.
3 Whisk the egg whites until stiff, then fold in a spoonful to the cheese sauce to loosen, then fold in the remaining whites. Divide the mixture between the ramekins and bake for 8-10 mins, until risen and golden.
4 Leave to cool; they will sink but don't panic! Carefully loosen and turn soufflés out into individual heatproof dishes or one dish.
5 Pour the cream over each soufflé and sprinkle with the remaining cheese. Bake at 200°C/400°F for 6 mins until golden and risen. Serve with watercress.

Squash, Pickled Beetroot and Burrata Salad

Burrata is an Italian cheese similar to mozzarella, and is also made from buffalo milk, but has a creamier centre and goes really well in this dish

Serves 4 * Ready in 1 hour

* 400g (14oz) cherry tomatoes, halved
* Olive oil spray
* 1 butternut squash, sliced into discs
* 10 cooked baby beetroot, halved

FOR THE PICKLE:
* 250g (9oz) sugar
* 100ml (3½fl oz) white wine vinegar
* 1tsp mustard seeds
* 1tsp coriander seeds
* 1tbsp fresh dill, chopped

To serve:
* 1 burrata
* Bunch of basil

1 Heat the air fryer to 200°C/400°F. Put the tomatoes in a bowl, spray with oil, season then air fry for 10 mins, shaking halfway through. Set aside. Spray the squash discs with oil, season, then air fry for 15 mins, shaking halfway through.
2 To make the pickle, combine all the ingredients with 500ml (16fl oz) water in a pan. Bring to the boil, then reduce the heat and simmer for 10 mins. Add the beetroot, increase the heat, and cook for a further 15 mins.
3 On a large platter, arrange the tomatoes, squash and beetroots removed from the pickling liquid. To serve, place the burrata in the centre, and pick and scatter over the basil leaves.

Indian Spiced King Prawns

These make fantastic party food to share dipped in mango chutney for that authentic Indian flavour

Serves 2 as a starter, or 6 as a pre-lunch nibble * Ready in 5 minutes, plus marinating

* 350g (12oz) jumbo king prawns, peeled
* 5tbsp hot curry paste, such as Rogan Josh
* Oil spray
* 3tbsp fresh coriander, chopped
* 4tbsp mango chutney

1 Mix the prawns with the curry paste and marinate in the fridge for 2-3 hrs.
2 Heat the air fryer to 180°C/350°F. Spray the prawns with oil, then air fry on a parchment liner for 4 mins, shaking halfway through.
3 Scatter with the coriander. Serve with the mango chutney to dip, with some mini poppadoms on the side.

Posh Mushrooms on Toast

A quick starter which would also make an indulgent festive brunch dish

Serves 4 * Ready in 20 minutes

* 125g (4oz) smoked bacon lardons
* 4 slices sourdough bread
* 8 Portobello mushrooms
* Olive oil spray
* 150g (5oz) fresh basil pesto
* 125g (4oz) ball mozzarella, torn
* Bag mixed salad, to serve

1 Heat the air fryer to 200°C/400°F. Cook the bacon lardons for 8 mins, shaking the basket halfway through, until crisp. Toast the bread for 2 mins a side in the air fryer, then air fry the mushrooms with a spray of oil for 3 mins. Put the mushrooms, gills upwards, on a parchment liner. Add the lardons, 1tbsp pesto to each and the mozzarella, pushing it down firmly.
2 Air fry the mushrooms for 3-4 mins until the filling is hot and bubbling. Serve on the toasts with a little salad on the side.

Beetroot and Goat's Cheese Herby Crostini

Serve these as a little pre-lunch canapé, rather than a classic starter. The crostini bases will keep for a few hours in an airtight container

Serves 4-6 * **Ready in 10 minutes**

* 1 baguette
* Oil spray
* 200g (7oz) soft goat's cheese or garlic and herb cream cheese
* 200g (7oz) cooked beetroot, cut into small chunks
* Orange zest and fresh thyme leaves, to serve

1 Heat the air fryer to 200°C/400°F. Slice the baguette into 16 slices. Spray with oil, then air fry for 4 mins, shaking halfway through, until crisp.
2 Spread the cheese over each one, top with the beetroot then scatter over the orange and thyme to serve.

"Serve these as a little pre-lunch canapé"

Loaded Mini Jackets

These toppings are a fab way to jazz up your spuds, and miniature potatoes make for a fantastic canapé

Serves 6-8 * Ready 1 hour

* 1kg (2lb 3oz) baby potatoes
* 2tbsp salted butter
* 2tbsp double cream
* Oil spray

FOR THE CRAB FILLING:
* 1 dressed crab
* 2tbsp crème fraîche
* 1 red chilli, chopped

FOR THE CHEESE AND BACON FILLING:
* 80g (3oz) mature Cheddar, grated
* 200g (7oz) smoked bacon lardons
* 3 spring onions, finely sliced

1 Boil the potatoes for 20-25 mins, until cooked but firm. Leave to cool.
2 Heat the air fryer to 200°C/400°F. Cook the bacon lardons for 8 mins, shaking halfway through, until crisp. Set aside. Halve the cooled potatoes, and scoop out the centre of the flesh – we did this using a melon baller. Put what you have scooped out into a small bowl, add the butter and cream, and mash with a fork. Spray the skins with oil and toss well. Bake them on a parchment liner in batches, for 10 mins.
3 To make the fillings, divide the mashed potato middles between 2 bowls. Add the crab filling ingredients to one bowl, and the cheese and bacon filling to another and blitz with a hand blender until combined. Fill half the crispy potato skins with the crab filling and half with the bacon and cheese, garnished with chopped chilli and spring onion.

57

"If you don't have chutney, drizzle
the cheese toasts with honey"

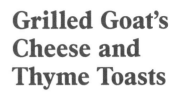

Grilled Goat's Cheese and Thyme Toasts

Keep portions small as this is quite rich

Serves 4 * **Ready in 10 minutes**

* 1 small baguette, cut into 4
* Olive oil spray
* 4tbsp fruity chutney
* 4 thick slices of soft goat's cheese
* 1 small bunch of thyme, leaves removed
* Salad leaves, to serve

1 Heat the air fryer to 200°C/400°F. Spray the bread slices with oil and air fry for 2 mins, flipping halfway through.
2 Remove from the air fryer and spread 1tbsp chutney on each piece of toasted baguette, then top with goat's cheese (pushing it into the chutney) and sprinkle with thyme leaves. Bake for a further 3-4 mins until just toasted and softened. Serve with the salad.

Pickled Mustard Seeds with Trout and Crème Fraîche Toasts

Pickled mustard seeds swell and soften as they cook, and pop like peppery caviar when eaten. Simple, light and elegant, these toasts are ideal for serving as a starter or canapés

Serves 4 as a starter ∗ **Ready in 25 minutes, plus 12-24hrs pickling**

FOR THE PICKLED MUSTARD SEEDS:
* 200g (7oz) yellow mustard seeds
* 350ml (12fl oz) cider vinegar, plus extra to taste
* 3tbsp golden caster sugar
* 1tsp sea salt flakes
* 2tsp ground turmeric
* 1tsp (heaped) finely grated fresh ginger

FOR THE TROUT TOASTS:
* 250g (9oz) trout fillets
* Oil spray
* 4 slices rustic bread, toasted and halved
* 100g (3½oz) crème fraîche
* 1tsp Dijon mustard, or to taste
* 2tbsp mustard cress leaves, snipped

1 To make the pickled mustard seeds, rinse the seeds in a sieve and shake well to drain, then transfer to a non-metallic bowl and cover with the vinegar. Set aside in a cool place (not the fridge) for at least 12 hrs or up to 24 hrs. Stir in the sugar, salt and turmeric. Squeeze the grated ginger over to release the juices, then discard the pulp.
2 Put the mixture in a saucepan and bring to the boil over a medium heat, then stir constantly, for about 15 mins, as it simmers and thickens. Remove from the heat and set aside to cool. Taste the mixture and add more vinegar, a little at a time, until it has a good, balanced vinegary tang. Cover and keep in the fridge for up to 6 months, adding a little extra vinegar if the mixture becomes too thick.
3 Heat the air fryer to 180°C/350°F. Spray the trout fillets with oil and season. Cook on parchment liners for 5 mins. Set aside to cool, then flake. To make the toasts, stir the crème fraîche and Dijon mustard together and season with salt and pepper. Spoon a little of the mixture onto each piece of toast with a couple pieces of trout, half a teaspoon of pickled mustard seeds and a scattering of cress.

Moroccan Sweet Potato Salad

Packed with flavour, this makes a lovely vegetarian starter, or a good salad for a festive buffet

Serves 6 * **Ready in 40 minutes**

* 2 x 400g (14oz) tins chickpeas, drained and rinsed
* Olive oil spray
* 4 sweet potatoes, cut into wedges
* 125g (4½oz) baby spinach leaves
* 90g (3½oz) rocket leaves
* 200g (7oz) feta cheese, broken into cubes
* 200g (7oz) mixed cherry tomatoes, chopped in half
* 200g (7oz) sun-dried tomatoes (from a jar), drained of their oil

FOR THE DRESSING:
* 3tbsp tahini
* Juice of half a lemon
* 1tbsp olive oil

1 Heat the air fryer to 200°C/400°F. Spray the chickpeas with oil, add plenty of sea salt, then cook for 10 mins, shaking the draw a few times. Set aside. Spray the sweet potatoes with oil, season and air fry for 15 mins, shaking a few times.
2 Arrange the spinach and rocket leaves on a large platter. Tumble over the roasted chickpeas and the sweet potatoes. Top with the feta cheese, cherry tomatoes, and sun-dried tomatoes.
3 To make the dressing mix the tahini, lemon juice and oil and then drizzle over the prepared salad before serving.

Scallop and Lobster Gratin

You could make a big portion of this for Christmas Eve too

Serves 4 * **Ready in 25 mins, plus infusing the milk**

* 150ml (5fl oz) milk
* 3 bay leaves
* 5 peppercorns
* ½ onion, left in one piece
* 30g (1oz) butter
* 2tbsp flour
* 250ml (8fl oz) double cream
* 100g (3½oz) grated mature Cheddar
* 4tbsp breadcrumbs
* 200g (7oz) lobster meat (raw or cooked)
* 250g (9oz) raw scallops

1 Put the milk, bay leaves, peppercorns and onion into a pan and heat gently, then set aside for 1 hr to infuse. Strain into a jug. Melt the butter, stir in the flour, then gradually whisk in the milk. Cook until thickened. Now whisk in the cream and half the cheese.
2 Heat the air fryer to 160°C/300°F. Divide the seafood between 4 ovenproof dishes or one shallow dish. Pour over the sauce. Mix together the breadcrumbs and remaining cheese, and sprinkle over the seafood. Push the topping down with a spoon to prevent it blowing around in the fan. Bake for 15 mins then increase the heat to 200°C/400°F and bake for a further 3 mins.

Cook's tip
This recipe is just as delicious made with king prawns instead of the lobster and scallops.

"Prepare the day
before and leave
covered in the
fridge overnight"

Twice-baked Smoked Salmon Soufflés

Elegant and delicious, and so much easier than you may think, made speedy in an air fryer

Serves 8 ∗ Ready in 25 minutes

- 50g (2oz) butter
- 50g (2oz) plain flour
- 300ml (½pt) milk
- 4 eggs, separated
- 50g (2oz) grated Gruyère cheese
- 100g (3½oz) smoked salmon trimmings

FOR THE SECOND BAKE:
- 200ml (7fl oz) double cream
- 75g (3oz) finely grated Gruyère cheese
- 8 small slices of smoked salmon and fresh dill, to serve

You will need:
8 small metal pudding basins, brushed with melted butter

1 Heat the air fryer to 200°C/400°F. Melt the butter in a saucepan then stir in the flour and cook for a few mins without letting it brown.

2 Gradually whisk in the milk and cook until it thickens. Let it cool for a few mins, then whisk in the egg yolks. Add the Gruyère and the smoked salmon trimmings. Beat the egg whites until stiff. Add a spoonful of this to the flour mix to loosen, then fold in the rest. Divide between the basins, leaving 1cm (½in) to rise.

3 Bake for 8-10 mins until risen and browned. Remove from the air fryer. They will sink but don't worry!

4 Remove from the basins and pop each into an ovenproof dish which fits your air fryer. Pour over the cream and sprinkle over the Gruyère. Bake for 6 mins until the cheese has melted. Serve each topped with smoked salmon and dill.

Pear, Goat's Cheese and Chicory Salad

An elegant salad that couldn't be easier to make. We melt the cheese in a hot, but switched off air fryer, so there's no chance it can blow away in the fan!

Serves 6 * **Ready in 15 minutes**

* 3 pears
* Juice of 1 lemon
* 150g (5oz) soft goat's cheese
* 3 slices white bread
* 2 heads red chicory
* 3tbsp orange blossom honey
* Fresh thyme leaves

1 Heat the air fryer to 200°C/400°F. Halve, then cut the pears into wedges. Toss in the lemon juice and set aside. Slice the goat's cheese into 6 thick slices. Toast one side of the bread in the air fryer for a min. Leave the air fryer on for the next step. Cut out circles or shapes (we did Christmas trees!) from the bread a little larger than the cheese slices.

2 Put a slice of cheese on each untoasted side of the bread. Arrange the chicory leaves on 6 plates. Add the pear slices. When ready to serve, switch off the air fryer and put the toasts in for 3-4 mins – the heat will be enough to melt the cheese. Put on the salad, drizzle with honey and sprinkle over the thyme.

65

Brie and Sweet Onion Tarts

What's not to love about these sweet and savoury little tarts?

Makes 6 * **Ready in 50 minutes**

* 2tbsp olive oil
* 3 large sweet onions, peeled and thinly sliced
* Few sprigs thyme, leaves only
* 375g (13oz) ready-rolled puff pastry
* 1 egg, beaten
* 2tbsp redcurrant jelly
* 200g (7oz) firm Brie, sliced
* 100g (3½oz) winter salad leaves

FOR THE DRESSING:
* 2tsp Dijon mustard
* 3tbsp olive oil
* 2tbsp lemon juice
* Pinch of sugar

1 Add the olive oil, onions and most of the thyme to a large pan. Gently cook over a low heat for about 30-40 mins until onions are very soft and light golden. Stir often, so they don't catch, season well and leave to cool.
2 Cut out six rounds of pastry, each one 10cm (4in) in diameter. Transfer to a lightly greased baking tray, brush with beaten egg and then score a 1cm (½in) border around the edge with a sharp knife, but not cutting right through the pastry. Prick the centres with a fork. Spread the centre of each round with onion, then add a few little blobs of redcurrant jelly (about 1tsp each) into the middle. Heat the air fryer to 190°C/375°F.

3 Bake for 5 mins, then add a few slices of Brie, pushing it into the onion so it doesn't blow off in the air fryer. Scatter over remaining thyme leaves and bake again for 3-4 mins.
4 To make the dressing, whisk all the ingredients together, then chill until required. Remove the tarts from the air fryer and cool for a few mins before serving with the salad leaves and a drizzle of dressing.

Cook's tip
Save time and effort by using a jar of onion marmalade for the filling.

Thai Spiced Pumpkin Soup

The flavourful toppings make this soup a bit more special

Serves 6 * Ready in 40 minutes

* 600g (1lb 5oz) pumpkin, peeled, deseeded and diced
* 2tbsp sunflower oil
* 4 small Thai shallots or 2 normal shallots
* A thumb-sized piece of fresh ginger, peeled and finely sliced
* 2 lemongrass sticks, trimmed and sliced
* 2 red chillies: 1 deseeded and roughly chopped; 1 finely sliced
* 2 garlic cloves
* 450ml (15fl oz) light coconut milk
* 350ml (12fl oz) vegetable stock
* Light soy sauce, ground black pepper and lime juice, to taste

To serve:
* A handful of cashew nuts, toasted and crushed
* Small handful coriander sprigs
* 2tbsp crispy fried shallots

1 Heat the air fryer to 180°C/350°F. Toss the pumpkin with the oil, shallots, ginger, lemongrass, roughly chopped chilli and garlic cloves in a heatproof dish which fits the air fryer. Cover tightly with foil (secure with string if needs be) and roast for 25 mins, until very tender.

2 Tip half the pumpkin into a blender with the coconut milk and blitz until very smooth. Pour into a large saucepan. Blitz the remaining pumpkin mixture with the vegetable stock. Add this to the first batch and stir well.

3 Put the pan over a low heat and gently bring to the boil, stirring often. Simmer gently for 5 mins then season to taste with the soy sauce, black pepper and lime juice.

4 Divide the soup between warmed bowls and scatter with the toasted cashews, coriander sprigs, sliced chilli and crispy fried shallots (if using) just before eating.

Irish Oat and Potato Cakes with Smoked Salmon

Hard to resist and best of all, these can be made the day before serving and then reheated

Serves 6 * **Ready in 35 minutes, plus chilling**

FOR THE HERBY CRÈME FRAÎCHE:
* Small bunch dill
* Small bunch parsley
* 1tbsp capers
* 1tbsp extra virgin olive oil
* ½ green chilli, deseeded and sliced
* Zest and juice of 1 lemon
* 150ml (5fl oz) crème fraîche

Just before cooking the potato cakes, make the green crème fraîche. Blend all the ingredients, except for the crème fraîche, in a food processor. Spoon the crème fraîche into a bowl and lightly ripple half the green mixture through. Spoon the remaining green sauce into a bowl.

FOR THE POTATO CAKES WITH SMOKED SALMON:
* 450g (1lb) baking potatoes, peeled and cut into large chunks
* 100g (3½oz) plain flour, plus extra for kneading
* 3tbsp oats
* 1tsp onion powder
* 1tsp sea salt
* 1 egg yolk
* Zest of 1 lemon, plus extra zest and lemon wedges, to serve
* ½ green chilli, finely chopped
* 60g (2½oz) butter, melted
* Olive oil spray
* 200g (7oz) smoked salmon

1 Simmer the potatoes in a pan of water for 15 mins. Drain and cool in a colander.
2 Mix the flour, oats, onion powder, salt, egg yolk, lemon zest, chilli, melted butter and potatoes together to form a soft dough. Knead on a lightly floured surface.
3 Shape the dough into 6 rounds, cover and chill for 30 mins or until ready to cook.
4 Heat the air fryer to 200°C/400°F. Spray the potato cakes with oil, and cook for 10 mins, then flip, spray again, and cook for a further 6 mins. Serve with the smoked salmon, herby crème fraîche, green sauce and lemon wedges.

MAINS

**WITH THESE RECIPES THE MAIN ACT WILL
CERTAINLY BE THE STAR OF THE SHOW**

Brussels Sprout Gratin

This is rich and creamy, a treat for a festive lunch

Serves 6-8 * **Ready in 30 minutes**

FOR THE GRATIN:
* 600g (1lb 5oz) Brussels sprouts, trimmed and cut in half or quartered if large
* 2 shallots, finely diced
* 1 garlic clove, crushed
* 4 thyme sprigs
* 500ml (16fl oz) double cream
* 60g (2½oz) Gruyère cheese, grated

FOR THE HERBY CRUMB:
* 3 slices sourdough bread
* 3 sprigs rosemary, leaves removed
* 3 sprigs thyme, leaves removed
* 1tbsp olive oil
* 30g (1oz) dried cranberries, roughly chopped

1 Heat the air fryer to 160°C/300°F. Add the sprouts to an ovenproof dish which fits your air fryer, around 20cm (8in) square usually. Add the shallots, garlic and thyme to a small pan with the double cream and simmer for 5 mins, being careful not to let it boil. Pour the cream over the Brussels sprouts, stir to coat and then top with the cheese. Air fry for 15 mins.
2 Meanwhile, blitz the sourdough, herbs, oil and a pinch of salt in a food processor to create breadcrumbs. Remove the gratin and spoon over the breadcrumbs, pushing them down with a fish slice. Return to the air fryer for another 5 mins. Sprinkle over the cranberries before serving.

Brown Butter and Sage Roast Potatoes

Air frying roast potatoes uses far less oil than a conventional oven

Serves 4 * Ready in 40 minutes

* 1kg (2lb 5oz) roasting potatoes, peeled and cut into chunks
* 1 garlic bulb, halved across the middle
* 2tbsp olive oil
* 50g (2oz) butter
* Small bunch sage, leaves picked
* ½tsp cumin seeds, optional

1 Steam the potatoes until just tender. Drain and steam-dry for 5 mins, then give the colander a good shake to rough up the edges. Heat the air fryer to 190°C/375°F.
2 Toss the potatoes and garlic in the oil with plenty of sea salt. Roast for 20 mins, shaking the basket occasionally. Put the potatoes in a foil tray. Increase the air fryer to 200°C/400°F.
3 Meanwhile, melt the butter in a small pan. Once foaming, add the sage and cumin seeds, and

continue to cook until the butter browns and smells nutty, and the sage is crispy. Set aside.
4 Drizzle the brown butter over the potatoes, reserving the sage, then return to the air fryer for another 10 mins until crisp and golden. Season with more salt and pepper, and serve sprinkled with the crispy sage leaves.

Roast Pork, Shallots and Apples

Air fryer pork belly is the best ever! It cooks in far less time, gives perfect crackling and there's no large oven to clean

Serves 8 * Ready in 2 hours 20 minutes, plus overnight marinating

* 1½kg (3lb) pork belly joint, skin scored
* ½ bulb garlic, cloves chopped
* ½tsp each juniper and allspice
* 1 bunch thyme, leaves picked
* 6 sprigs rosemary, leaves picked
* Zest 1 orange
* 5 large banana shallots, halved
* Handful sage leaves
* Opies pickled pears, optional

You will need:
Kitchen string

1 Unroll the pork belly. Combine the garlic, spices, herbs and zest. Rub all over the meat and under the skin, then roll up and tie with kitchen string in intervals to secure the joint. We suggest getting an extra pair of hands to assist with the tying. Put on a tray uncovered in the fridge (away from other foods) overnight to marinate and dry out the skin.

2 Heat the air fryer to 140°C/250°F. Make a triangle with two pieces of foil, then wrap the pork so that the top and small sides are covered, but not the long sides. Tuck it under the pork well, so the foil doesn't fly off in the fan. Roast for 2 hrs, then remove the foil, turn up the heat to 200°C/400°F, and roast for 15 mins or until the crackling is brown and crisp.

3 Let the pork rest, then remove the crackling, using scissors to cut into chunks. Slice the pork thinly and serve with the trimmings and pickled pears, if using.

Pigs in Blanket Stuffing Wreath

A cute centrepiece showcasing a different way to serve stuffing and pigs in blankets

Serves 6 * Ready in 1 hour

FOR THE STUFFING:
* 1tbsp oil
* 2 red onions, finely chopped
* 1tbsp balsamic vinegar
* 450g (1lb) sausage meat
* 4 sprigs of thyme, leaves removed
* 5tbsp fresh breadcrumbs
* 1 egg, beaten
* Pinch of nutmeg, optional

* 20 cocktail sausages
* 10 rashers of streaky bacon

To serve:
* Cranberry sauce, optional
* Sprigs of thyme, to decorate

You will also need:
A 20cm (8in) loose-bottomed cake tin; a small ramekin or metal pudding dish, well greased

1 Heat 1tbsp oil in a frying pan and fry the onion for 10 mins until softened. Add the balsamic vinegar, cook for 1 min then transfer to a mixing bowl to cool. Mix in the remaining stuffing ingredients.
2 Put the ramekin in the centre of the tin then press the stuffing into the space around it.
3 Stretch the bacon with the back of a knife. Wrap a piece around each sausage. Arrange in a ring on top of the stuffing around the edge of the tin. Heat the air fryer to 160°C/300°F. Bake the wreath for 25 mins, then increase the heat to 180°C/350°F and bake for a further 10 mins.
4 Transfer the wreath to a serving plate. Fill the ramekin with cranberry sauce and garnish with herbs.

Cheesy Sage and Lemon Hasselback Potatoes

These are well worth a little extra effort for a special occasion

Serves 6 * Ready in 45 minutes

* **600g (1lb 5oz) new potatoes**
* **1tbsp olive oil**
* **15g (½oz) butter,**
  plus extra for frying
* **3tbsp Parmesan cheese,**
  finely grated
* **10 sage leaves**
* **1tbsp lemon olive oil**
* **Zest of 1 lemon**

1 Heat the air fryer to 180°C/350°F. Slice your potatoes into hasselbacks. The easiest way to do this is to place the potato between two chopsticks – this way your knife won't go all the way through. Make the slices approximately 3-5mm (⅛-¼in) apart.
2 Mix together the oil and melted butter. Toss the potatoes well in them and season with salt. Air fry, cut side up, for 25 mins. After 20 mins, sprinkle over 1tbsp of the cheese.

3 Meanwhile, melt some more butter in a frying pan and fry the sage leaves until crisp. Drain on some kitchen towel, until ready to serve.
4 Once the potatoes are cooked, drizzle over the lemon oil, lemon zest and remaining cheese. Spoon into a serving dish and scatter over the crispy sage leaves.

Sweet Potato Star Gratin

A flavour-packed meat-free main course which can be cooked ahead of time, then reheated. Slice the potatoes with a mandolin or food processor

Serves 2 * Ready in 1 hour

* 450g (1lb) sweet potato, peeled, cut into thin slices (set some aside, and cut into stars)
* 50g (2oz) chestnuts, roasted and peeled
* 15g (½oz) butter
* 4tbsp chestnut purée
* 5tbsp double cream
* 5tbsp vegetable stock
* 4 sprigs fresh thyme, leaves stripped
* 60g (2½oz) vegetarian hard cheese, such as Cheddar
* 2tbsp breadcrumbs

1 Arrange the sweet potato in an ovenproof dish in rows, overlapping a little. Scatter half of the chestnuts over the top and repeat. Melt the butter in a pan and whisk in the chestnut purée. Add the cream, stock and thyme to warm through. Season, then pour over the sweet potatoes and chestnuts. Heat the air fryer to 160°C/300°F.

2 Sprinkle with half the cheese, cover tightly with foil then cook for 20 mins. Uncover, add the remaining cheese and breadcrumbs and press down with a fish slice. Cook for a further 20 mins until golden brown and bubbling.

Stuffed Butternut Squash

A veggie main with a difference, roasted and stuffed whole squash. Ensure you buy two squash which will fit into your air fryer

Serves 8 * Ready in 1 hour 30 minutes

* 2 x butternut squash
* 1 onion, diced
* ½tbsp olive oil
* 75g (3oz) spinach
* 100g (3½oz) Brussels sprouts, shredded
* 250g (9oz) microwaveable mixed grain pouch
* 1tsp balsamic vinegar
* 150g (5oz) soft goat's cheese
* 1tbsp chopped pecan nuts

1 Cut each butternut squash in half lengthways and hollow out the seeds, then use a spoon to scoop out a 2cm (¾in) deep cavity the length of each half.
2 Sweat the onion in the oil until soft and golden. Mix in the spinach, sprouts, grains and vinegar, and season. Stir until the spinach is wilted.
3 Off the heat, mix in the cheese and nuts, and press the mixture into the cavities on each side of the squash. Put both sides together, tie up with string then chill them. You need to tie them up tightly, so grab another pair of hands. Otherwise the fan in the air fryer will blow the sides apart.
4 When you are ready to cook, heat the air fryer to 180°C/350°F. Bake the squash on a liner for 1 hr.

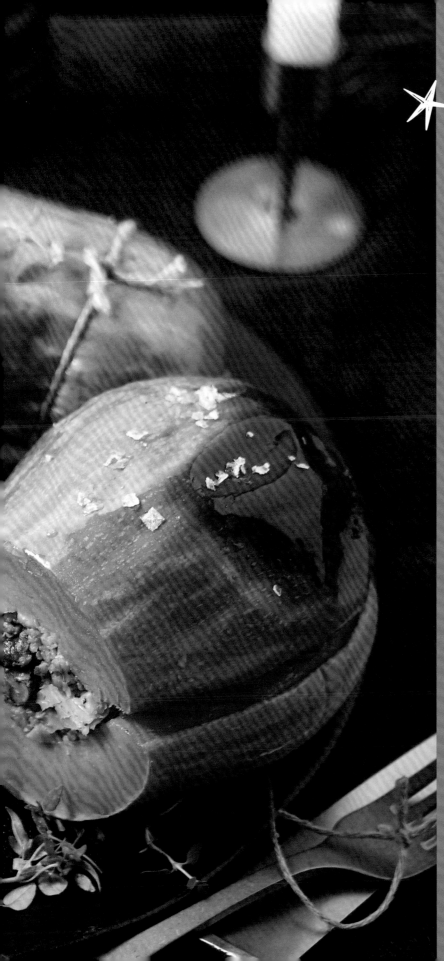

Toasted Bread Sauce

Toasting the bread first adds flavour and texture

Serves 8 * **Ready in 30 minutes**

* 2 slices sourdough bread
* 600ml (20fl oz) milk
* 1 onion, halved
* 1 bay leaf
* ½tsp whole peppercorns
* Pinch of nutmeg
* 3tbsp double cream

1 Heat the air fryer to 180°C/350°F. Toast the bread in the air fryer for 2 mins a side, leave it to cool and then blitz into breadcrumbs.
2 Add the milk, onion, bay leaf, peppercorns and nutmeg to a pan with a pinch of salt. Bring up to a very gentle simmer for 20 mins before straining out the aromatics and returning the milk to the pan. Stir in the breadcrumbs and simmer for 2-3 mins until the sauce has thickened slightly. Stir through the double cream, heat through and serve.

Cook's tip
Furikake is a Japanese rice seasoning, but it's great on vegetables.

Charred Sweetheart Cabbage with Miso

A delicious and modern take on cabbage. Buy the right size so that the eight wedges of cabbage will fit your air fryer at the same time

Serves 8 • Ready in 30 minutes

* 2 sweetheart cabbages (also known as pointed or hispi)
* 4tbsp olive oil
* 150g (5oz) butter, softened
* 45g (1½oz) organic gluten-free miso paste
* 2 garlic cloves, crushed

FOR THE DRESSING:
* 4tbsp tahini
* 1tbsp sesame oil
* 1tbsp maple syrup
* 1tsp ginger, minced
* Furikake sesame seed seasoning, to garnish, optional

1 Heat a griddle pan on high. Cut the cabbages in half and divide in half again, or thirds, depending on the size. Leave as much as you can of the core so they remain intact. Brush the cut sides with oil and place on the griddle pan for around 6 mins before repeating on the other side. You want it well charred.
2 Line the air fryer basket with foil, or use a parchment liner with sides. Heat the air fryer to 170°C/325°F. Mix the butter, miso and garlic together, and spread all over the charred cabbage, making sure to get into all of the nooks and crannies. Roast for 15 mins (depending on size), basting halfway through. Once cooked, transfer to a serving platter.
3 For the dressing, whisk all the ingredients together with 2tbsp water, and pour over the cabbage. Garnish with furikake seasoning, if using.

Roast Parmesan and Lemon Sprouts

An easy update to a traditional dish gives these sprouts a wonderful flavour

Serves 4 • Ready in 25 minutes

* 450g (1lb) Brussels sprouts, trimmed and halved
* 1tbsp olive oil
* ½tsp chilli flakes
* 1tbsp Parmesan, finely grated
* Zest and juice 1 lemon

1 Heat the air fryer to 160°C/325°F. Toss the sprouts, oil and chilli flakes together. Season with some salt, and air fry for 15 mins until slightly caramelised. Increase the heat to 180°C/350°F.
2 Stir in the Parmesan and lemon zest, and cook for a further 5 mins until the cheese is golden and the sprouts are tender.
3 Serve with a squeeze of lemon juice and extra zest if you like.

"Vegan Parmesan can be
substituted for dairy-free guests"

Stuffed Turkey Breast

Save time and free up oven space by cooking a succulent joint of turkey in the air fryer. Ensure you know the dimensions of your air fryer before buying the turkey, so that it fits

Serves 8 * **Ready in 1 hour 30 minutes, plus resting**

* 1½-1¾kg (3-3½lb) turkey breast or crown, butterflied (ask your butcher to do this)
* 16-20 rashers streaky bacon

FOR THE STUFFING:
* 350g (12oz) sausage meat
* 2 sprigs rosemary, leaves picked, finely chopped
* 3 sprigs thyme, leaves picked
* Handful parsley, finely chopped
* 2tbsp caramelised red onion chutney
* 3tbsp breadcrumbs

1 Mix all the stuffing ingredients together. You can do this ahead of time and leave, covered, in the fridge.
2 Heat the air fryer to 180°C/350°F. Put an air fryer liner with sides under the basket to catch the juices and make cleaning easier. Open the butterflied turkey breast out like a book. Arrange the stuffing along the centre of the opened breast like a sausage. Fold over the bottom flap to enclose the stuffing and turn the right side up.
3 Wrap the turkey in the bacon, overlapping the slices, then tie with kitchen string a few times along the length of the breast.
4 Roast the turkey, skin side down, for 40 mins. Flip it over and roast for a further 30 mins. The internal temperature should be 65°C/150°F. Once cooked through, allow it to rest for 10 mins before carving.

Cook's tip

If the bacon is browning too quickly, wrap the turkey in foil, tucking it underneath to keep it in place, or the fan may blow it off.

Pigs in Blankets

Air-fried sausages wrapped in bacon take no time to cook and will free up space in the main oven if you're roasting a large turkey

Makes 16 ♦ Ready in 20 minutes

* **16 rashers of smoked streaky bacon**
* **32 sage leaves**
* **16 pork chipolatas**

1 Lay the bacon on a chopping board and run the back of a knife along the length of each rasher to stretch it. Put the sage leaves, 2 per rasher, on top and roll up a chipolata with the bacon. Repeat.
2 Put a parchment liner under the basket to catch any fat and make cleaning easier. Heat the air fryer to 180°C/350°F. Cook the sausages for 7 mins, then flip and cook for a further 7 mins. If the sausages are quite thick, add 2 mins per side extra.

"Add toothpicks to make these a party snack"

Whisky Marmalade Glazed Ham

No faffing around with boiling, a ham works perfectly baked in the air fryer, and doesn't dry out

Serves 4-6 * **Ready in 1 hour 50 minutes**

* 1½kg (3lb) boneless gammon joint, smoked or unsmoked

FOR THE GLAZE:
* 3tbsp thick-cut marmalade
* 2tbsp whisky
* 2tsp English mustard powder

"**Make this the star of your Boxing Day buffet**"

1 Wrap the ham, skin side up, in a double layer of foil, scrunching up the top to make a parcel, but leaving enough space for air to circulate. Mix the glaze ingredients together.
2 Heat the air fryer to 170°C/325°F. Bake the ham for 1 hr 10 mins. (Now remove any netting). Peel back the foil, brush the glaze over the skin and bake for a further 25 mins. The ham should show 60°C/140°F on a meat thermometer when cooked through. Leave to rest for 10-15 mins before carving.

Boulangère Potatoes

A lovely way with potatoes, which can be baked ahead of time, then reheated to serve. Use a mandolin or food processor to slice the potatoes

Serves 2-3 * Ready in 1 hour 15 minutes

* 30g (1oz) butter
* 4 shallots, sliced
* 350g (12oz) floury potatoes
* 1 sprig of rosemary
* 200ml (7fl oz) hot chicken or vegetable stock
* Oil spray

You will need:
15cm (6in) round baking dish

1 Lightly butter the baking dish.
2 Heat the remaining butter in a small frying pan and cook the shallots, until soft and lightly golden – about 8 mins.
Heat the air fryer to 160°C/300°F.
3 Thinly slice the potatoes.
Layer up the potatoes and shallots in the dish, adding some rosemary leaves to each layer, seasoning as you go. Finish with a layer of potatoes and season. Pour over the hot stock. Push down the potatoes with a fish slice so they are all coated in stock. Cover tightly with foil and bake for 40 mins. Uncover, spray with oil and bake for a further 20 mins.

"For a rustic twist to the dish, leave the potatoes unpeeled"

Fennel and Herb Salmon en Croûte

A perfect, show-stopping main for those who don't eat meat. It can all be prepared the day before and left in the fridge

Serves 6 * **Ready in 40 minutes, plus chilling**

* **2 x 400g (14oz) salmon fillets, skinned**
* **450g (1lb) all-butter puff pastry**
* **1 egg, beaten**

FOR THE FILLING:
* **A knob of butter**
* **1 leek, finely chopped, white part only**
* **1 small fennel bulb, finely chopped**
* **1 garlic clove, finely chopped**
* **Zest and juice of 1 lemon**
* **100g (3½oz) spinach**
* **100g (3½oz) watercress**
* **3tbsp crème fraîche**
* **1 handful each of tarragon leaves, dill leaves and flat-leaf parsley, chopped**

1 Heat the butter in a frying pan and add the leek, fennel and garlic. Sauté until starting to soften; add the lemon juice and cook for another min. Add the spinach and watercress, cook for 30 secs, then transfer to a food processor with the crème fraîche, lemon zest, herbs and seasoning, and process until finely chopped.

2 Season the salmon, then spread the herb mixture over one side of one fillet and top with the other. Roll out the pastry on a floured surface and trim so it is big enough to leave a 2cm (¾in) border around the salmon when folded over. Place on a lined baking sheet and put the salmon on the top half. Fold the pastry over the fish, then seal edges with a fork. Brush with beaten egg and chill for 30 mins.

3 Heat the air fryer to 180°C/350°F. Cook the salmon on a parchment liner for 15 mins, then flip, glaze again and bake for a further 15 mins until browned and crisp all over. Rest for a few mins and then slice and serve.

Roasted Parsnips with Honey, Hazelnuts and Truffle Oil

Sweet, golden roasted parsnips are always a welcome side to a winter feast. These ones are made extra special with the crunch of hazelnuts and luxurious truffle oil

Serves 4 * Ready in 30 minutes

* **450g (1lb) parsnips, peeled and sliced lengthways into quarters**
* **Olive oil to drizzle**
* **2tbsp runny honey**
* **½ bunch of thyme, leaves only**
* **A handful of hazelnuts, roughly chopped**
* **A few drops of truffle oil**

1 Heat the air fryer to 180°C/350°F. Steam the parsnips for 5 mins. Then put the parsnips into a bowl, season with sea salt and pepper, drizzle over some olive oil and 2tbsp honey. Scatter over the thyme and toss to mix. Air fry on a liner for 15 mins until the parsnips are caramelised. Scatter over the hazelnuts and air fry for a further 2 mins.
2 Remove and arrange on a serving platter, drizzle over the remaining honey and a few drops of truffle oil. Serve at once.

Pork, Apple and Chestnut Stuffing

Classic flavours combine to give a delicious roast-dinner staple, cooked much quicker in the air fryer than a conventional oven

**Serves 6-8 ＊
Ready in 35 minutes**

＊ 30g (1oz) butter
＊ 2 large red onions, chopped
＊ Handful sage leaves, chopped
＊ 175g (6oz) cooked chestnuts, roughly chopped
＊ 2 slices sourdough bread, ripped into small chunks
＊ 400g (14oz) sausage meat
＊ 1 large cooking apple (approx 350g/12oz)
＊ 1 egg, beaten

1 Melt the butter in a frying pan, add the onions and cook for 5 mins. Stir through the chopped sage and cook for a further 5 mins or until the onions have softened. Set aside to cool.
2 In a large bowl, combine the chestnuts, sourdough and sausage meat. Peel, core and grate the apple, and mix into the sausage meat with the onion mixture. Season well and mix in the egg. You may want to use your hands to mix well.
3 Shape the stuffing into balls. It will keep in the fridge, covered, for a couple of days. To cook, heat the air fryer to 180°C/350°F and cook for 15 mins, turning halfway through so they are browned all over and cooked through.

Honey and Sesame Glazed Root Veg

The perfect balance of salty and sweet, this will bring your veg to centre stage

Serves 4 * Ready in 40 minutes

* 250g (9oz) carrots, peeled
* 250g (9oz) parsnips, peeled
* 1tbsp oil

FOR THE SAUCE:
* 1tbsp honey
* 1tbsp sesame oil
* 1tbsp soy sauce
* 1tbsp tomato purée
* 1tbsp sesame seeds, to garnish, optional

1 Line the air fryer with foil or use a liner with sides and no perforations. Heat the air fryer to 180°C/350°F. Cut the carrots and parsnips into 5cm (2in) chunks. Toss in the oil then spread onto the liner and cook for 15 mins.

2 Meanwhile, combine the sauce ingredients. Drizzle over the sauce and mix well to coat the veg. Season with pepper and return to the air fryer for a further 10 mins until tender, and the glaze is sticky and caramelised.

3 To serve, sprinkle with sesame seeds.

"Mash some of the roasted garlic into some butter to serve with bread at the table"

Roast Sirloin of Beef with Red Wine, Juniper Gravy and Horseradish Cream

Sirloin is full of flavour and cooks quite quickly in an air fryer. It does need to be served rare or medium rare, or it will dry out and become a little tough. The gravy can be prepared ahead of time, then reheated

Serves 6 * **Ready in 2 hours**

* 4 whole garlic heads
* 4tbsp olive oil
* 2 thyme sprigs, torn
* ¼tsp dried chilli flakes
* 1 x 1½kg (3lb) piece beef sirloin

FOR THE GRAVY:
* 2tbsp vegetable oil
* 2 celery stalks, cut into chunks
* 1 leek, white part only, cut into chunks
* 1 carrot, cut into chunks
* 2tbsp plain flour
* 2 bay leaves
* 10 juniper berries
* 250ml (8fl oz) red wine
* 2tsp soft brown sugar
* 500ml (16fl oz) beef stock
* 1tbsp Dijon mustard

FOR THE HORSERADISH CREAM:
* 5cm (2in) piece fresh horseradish, grated
* 200g (7oz) crème fraîche

1 For the gravy, put the vegetable oil in a large saucepan over a high heat. Add the celery, leek and carrot to the pan and season with salt and freshly ground black pepper. Lightly brown for about 5 mins. Then stir in the flour and cook, stirring regularly, for 2 mins, before adding the bay leaves and juniper berries. Pour in the red wine and bring to the boil, then reduce to a simmer, cooking until the liquid is reduced by one third.
2 Add the soft brown sugar and beef stock. Return to the boil and simmer for 15 mins to thicken and concentrate the flavours. Stir in the mustard, then strain into a clean saucepan and adjust the seasoning with salt and freshly ground black pepper. Set aside.
3 Heat the air fryer to 160°C/300°F. Cut the whole garlic heads in half. Sit them in a double layer of foil and drizzle with the olive oil. Season with salt and scatter with the thyme and dried chilli. Lift the foil over the garlic and scrunch up to seal into a parcel. Roast for 1 hr, open up the foil and roast for a further 5 mins. Set aside, still wrapped, while you cook the beef.
4 Rub the remaining oil over the beef and season with sea salt and freshly ground black pepper. Place a frying pan over a high heat. When the pan is very hot, sear the beef on all sides until it is browned. Increase the temperature of the air fryer to 200°C/400°F.
5 Roast the sirloin for 20 mins, reduce the heat to 180°C/350°F and roast for a further 5 mins. Leave to rest. For rare beef, it should read 50°C/120°F on a digital thermometer.
6 Just before serving, reheat the gravy and make the horseradish cream by stirring the grated horseradish into the crème fraîche and season with salt and pepper. Serve with the carved beef and roasted garlic.

99

DESSERTS & BAKES

IMPRESS FRIENDS AND FAMILY WITH THESE MOUTH-WATERING SWEET TREATS

Best Ever Gingerbread

This simple recipe will be your go-to for biscuits, Christmas tree decorations or even gift tags

Makes about 16-20 * **Ready in 20 minutes, plus chilling**

* 100g (3½oz) salted butter
* 3tbsp golden syrup
* 50g (2oz) dark muscovado sugar
* 50g (2oz) light muscovado sugar
* ¼tsp bicarbonate of soda
* 1tbsp ground ginger
* 1tsp ground mixed spice
* 225g (8oz) plain flour

You will need:
Festive cookie cutters
Air fryer pierced baking parchment liners

1 Melt the butter, golden syrup and both dark and light muscovado sugars in a pan over a medium heat, stirring until smooth. Sift in the remaining ingredients, then mix thoroughly to form a soft dough.
2 Flatten the dough into a disk. Roll the dough between two sheets of baking paper while still warm. It will cool faster and require less elbow grease to roll. Slide onto a tray and chill until firm.
3 Cut into shapes. Heat the air fryer to 170°C/325°F. Bake in batches on the liners for 10 mins, then cool on a wire rack.

"Make the dough the day before and leave in the fridge overnight for a stronger flavour"

Cook's tip
Gingerbread biscuits freeze well for up to a month. Thaw at room temperature.

Royal Icing

The trick to perfectly iced cookies is getting the icing consistency right. This recipe is very forgiving, so play around with the consistency, simply add a little more water if it's too stiff, or more icing sugar if too runny

Ready in 10 minutes

* 250g (9oz) icing sugar, sifted
* 1 egg white
* ½tsp lemon juice

You will need:
Electric hand whisk or food processor

1 Sift the icing sugar into a mixing bowl. Add the egg white and lemon juice, then whisk with an electric hand whisk on a low speed (you don't want too much air in the icing) for 2–3 mins or until it becomes a smooth, stiff peak consistency. It should be thick but spreadable. If it looks dry and crumbly, whisk in a few more drops of water. If it looks runny and glossy, mix in a little extra icing sugar.

2 Transfer to a bowl and cover with a damp cloth to prevent it from drying out. The icing will keep for up to 1 week, stored in an airtight container in the fridge. Use the icing as it is to stick gingerbread pieces together or thin with a little water for decorating biscuits.

Classic Christmas Cake

Fruit laden with a hint of ginger and spice make this a delicious cake. Best of all, it takes time to cook, so baking it in the air fryer frees up your main oven

Serves 20 * **Ready in 2 hours 15 minutes, plus soaking, cooling and decorating**

* 500g (1lb 2oz) mixed dried fruit
* 4 balls stem ginger in syrup, chopped
* 150ml (5fl oz) cherry brandy, plus extra for feeding
* 250g (9oz) unsalted butter, softened
* 200g (9oz) dark brown muscovado sugar
* 4 medium eggs
* 250g (9oz) plain flour
* 2tsp baking powder
* 150g (5oz) ground almonds
* 2tsp mixed spice

FOR THE MARZIPAN AND ICING:
* 2tbsp smooth apricot jam
* 500g (1lb 2oz) marzipan
* 1 egg white
* 250g (9oz) icing sugar, plus extra for dusting

You will need:
20cm (8in) tall-sided cake tin, the base and sides oiled then lined with 2 sheets of baking paper
Foil, to cover
Rolling pin

1 Put the dried fruit, stem ginger and brandy in a large mixing bowl, mix, then cover and set aside for 3 hrs or overnight.
2 Using an electric mixer, cream together the butter and sugar until lighter and creamy. Mix in the eggs, one at a time. Sift over the flour and baking powder, with the ground almonds and spice, then fold in, along with the soaked fruit. Heat the air fryer to 140°C/250°F.
3 Spoon the mixture into the lined tin. Level the top. Cover the top tightly with foil and secure with string (this prevents the fan blowing the foil off), then bake for 1 hr 30 mins. Fold back the foil and bake for a further 10 mins. Check it's cooked through by inserting a metal skewer into the centre, which should come out clean. Leave to cool in the tin. Transfer to a wire rack.
4 Poke holes into the top of the cake and pour over 1tbsp of extra brandy. Store well wrapped in the tin until ready to decorate. Repeat the feed every couple of weeks (a maximum of three times in total) until Christmas, to help preserve the cake and keep it moist.
5 To ice, trim the top of the cake to level. Warm the jam, then brush over the top and sides. On an icing-dusted worktop, roll out the marzipan to a circle large enough to cover the cake with some excess. Use a rolling pin to roll up the marzipan and unravel it over your cake, smooth out with your hands, then trim off and discard the excess.
6 For the royal icing, whisk the egg white until frothy in a stand mixer, and add the icing sugar and 1tsp water. Whisk for 5 mins until thick and glossy. Add more water if necessary. Use a palette knife to spread over the cake, creating a little texture.

Gingerbread Gift Tags

These sweet little decorations will add a real personal touch to your gift wrapping

Makes 20-30 * **Ready in 30 minutes, plus drying**

* **1 portion gingerbread dough, p102**
* **1 portion royal icing, p104**
* **Food colouring, preferably gel**

You will need:
Festive cookie cutters, piping bags

1 Roll out the gingerbread dough on a lightly floured surface to about 5mm (¼in) thickness. Use a sharp knife to cut the dough into small rectangles about 10 x 5cm (4 x 2in), then cut the corners off one end to fashion the dough into a gift tag shape. Alternatively, cut out any shape you prefer using festive cookie cutters such as Christmas trees or gingerbread men.

2 Use a 1cm (½in) piping nozzle or straw to punch out a hole in each cookie for threading later. Bake in the air fryer following the instructions for the gingerbread biscuits until firm and slightly darkened (they will harden as they cool). Cool on trays.

3 Divide the icing between two bowls. Adjust the consistency of one portion for piping and the other for flooding. Colour about one-third of the piping icing (we went Christmas red for ours), then transfer all three portions of icing to separate piping bags.

4 Snip the ends off the piping bags to make a very small hole and use the thicker white icing to pipe a border around the cookies and around the hole too. Set aside for 5 mins to harden a little, then use the thinner flooding icing to fill them in. Use a toothpick to spread the icing to create a smooth, thin and even layer. Set aside to dry for at least 1 hr.

5 Use the coloured icing to carefully write festive greetings onto the tags. Set aside to dry completely – at least 4 hrs or ideally overnight. Thread with ribbon or string and use to decorate your gifts.

Chocolate Coffee Brownie Mince Pies

A festive mince pie especially for chocolate lovers. Again, use silicone muffin cases if you don't have small metal muffin tins

Makes 12 * **Ready in 40 minutes, plus chilling**

FOR THE PASTRY:
* 215g (7½oz) plain flour
* 2tbsp icing sugar
* 125g (4oz) butter
* 1 egg

FOR THE FILLING:
* 75g (3oz) butter
* 100g (3½oz) dark chocolate
* 125g (4oz) light muscovado sugar
* 75g (3oz) plain flour
* ¼tsp baking powder
* 2tsp instant espresso coffee powder, mixed with 2tbsp boiling water
* 2 eggs, beaten
* 250g (9oz) mincemeat
* Icing sugar, to dust

You will need:
12 silicone muffin cases and a 10cm (4in) cutter

1 For the pastry, pulse the flour and sugar with the butter in a food processor until it resembles fine breadcrumbs. Add the egg and pulse until a dough is formed. Wrap in cling film and place in the fridge for 30 mins.
2 For the filling, melt the butter and chocolate in a heatproof bowl over simmering water. In a separate bowl, mix together the sugar, flour and baking powder. Stir in the melted butter mixture, espresso mix and eggs.
3 Roll the pastry out on a well-floured surface, to 3mm (just under ¼in) thickness. Using the cutter, cut out 12 rounds and press them into the cases. Heat the air fryer to 160°C/300°F.
4 Place a heaped tsp of the mincemeat into the base of each pie, then top with the brownie mixture. Fill the mixture to just below the pastry rim. Bake for 15 mins, then remove from the cases and bake for 5 mins (if using silicone). They should be puffed up and cooked through. Allow to cool before dusting with icing sugar and serving.

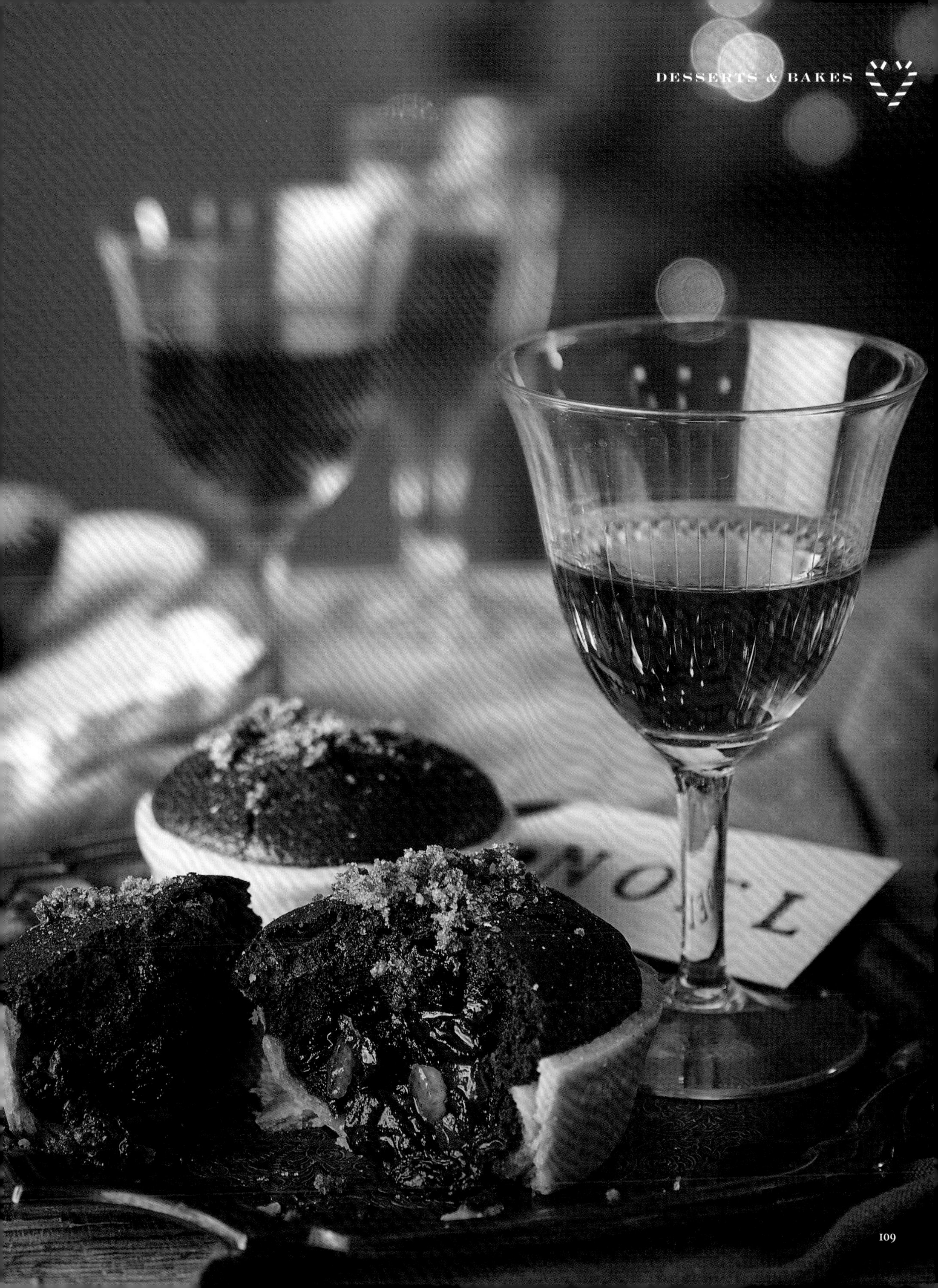

Apple and Cinnamon Crumble with Homemade Custard

Easy to make and a perfect warming pudding for a chilly day. Depending on the size of your air fryer and which dishes you have, you may need to make two separate ones

Serves 8 * Ready in 40 minutes

* 850g (1lb 14oz) cooking apples, peeled, cored and chopped
* Juice of 1 lemon
* 1 cinnamon stick
* 1tbsp golden caster sugar
* 90g (3oz) plain flour
* 2tbsp ground almonds
* 90g (3oz) cold salted butter, plus extra for dotting on top
* 3tbsp light muscovado sugar
* 90g (3oz) rolled oats
* A pinch of ground cinnamon

You will need:
A deep oval pie dish

1 Put the apples, lemon juice, cinnamon stick and sugar in a deep pan, cover and cook over a gentle heat for 8-10 mins until the apples begin to soften.
2 Put the flour, ground almonds and butter into a food processor and whizz until it forms breadcrumbs. Stir through the sugar, oats and cinnamon.

3 Heat the air fryer to 180°C/350°F. Remove the cinnamon stick from the apple and pour into the baking dish, top with the crumble, dot with extra butter and poke the cinnamon stick into the centre. Bake for 15-20 mins, until topping is golden brown.

FOR THE CUSTARD:
Take 600ml (1 pt) milk and 4tbsp single cream, and place in a saucepan with 1tsp vanilla extract. In a large bowl, mix together 4 egg yolks with 2tbsp caster sugar and 2tsp cornflour. Scald the milk then pour on to the egg mixture, stirring well. Return to the pan and, over a gentle heat, keep whisking gently with a balloon whisk until the custard has thickened and you see an almost jelly-like wobble. Pour into a warmed jug to serve.

Speculaas Biscuits

Festive spice and all things nice, these biscuits, popular in the Netherlands and Belgium, are delightful bites

Makes 20 * **Ready in 45 minutes**

* 100g (3½oz) unsalted butter, at room temperature
* 3tbsp plus 1tsp dark brown soft sugar
* 1tsp vanilla bean paste
* Zest of ½ an orange
* 1tsp dark rum
* 1tbsp plus 1tsp toasted flaked almonds
* ¼tsp white pepper
* Seeds from 2 cardamom pods
* ¼tsp nutmeg
* 2tsp mixed spice
* 1tsp ground ginger
* 200g (7oz) plain flour, plus extra for dusting

You will need:
Speculaas biscuit roller, springerle moulds or biscuit cutters

1 Cream the butter and sugar until light and fluffy, mix in the vanilla, orange zest and rum.
2 Blitz almonds with the white pepper and spices in a food processor until fine, then mix with the flour.
3 Mix the dry ingredients into the butter until just coming together. Tip out on to the worktop and mould into a ball. Wrap in cling film and refrigerate for 20 mins.
4 Heat the air fryer to 170°C/325°F. Dust the worktop with flour. Roll out the dough to a thickness of 3mm (⅛in). Dust it with a little flour and rub off. Press down firmly with the rolling pin and roll to indent the shapes. Use a knife to cut out the biscuits. Bake, in batches, for 10-12 mins until turning golden brown. Cool on a wire rack.

Coffee and Walnut Cake

This gluten-free loaf cake is rustled up pretty quickly, and freezes well without the buttercream

Serves 6 * **Ready in 40 minutes**

* 4 eggs
* 100g (3½oz) soft brown sugar
* 2tbsp olive oil
* 1tbsp cooled espresso coffee
* Zest of ½ orange
* 100g (3½oz) walnuts or walnut flour
* 50g (2oz) ground almonds
* ½tsp gluten-free baking powder
* 60g (2½oz) rice flour

FOR THE BUTTERCREAM:
* 100g (3½oz) butter, softened
* 150g (5oz) icing sugar
* 4tbsp cooled espresso coffee
* Walnuts, to decorate

You will need:
20 x 9cm (8 x 3½in) loaf tin, lined with baking parchment

1 Whisk the eggs, sugar, olive oil, coffee and orange zest until frothy.
2 If using whole walnuts, blitz in a food processor to a fine crumb. Fold the dry ingredients into the egg mixture and pour into the loaf tin. Heat the air fryer to 180°C/350°F. Cover the cake with foil, ensuring there's a little space for the cake to rise. You may want to secure the foil with string to prevent the fan blowing it off.
3 Bake for 15 mins, uncover and bake for a further 20 mins. Remove from the tin and transfer to a wire rack to cool.
4 For the buttercream, beat the butter until soft. Add the icing sugar, 1tbsp at a time. Mix until light and fluffy. Gradually incorporate the cold coffee, and mix until smooth.
5 Spread over the top of the cake and top with walnut halves.

Chocolate Torte with Baileys Cream and Salted Praline

Similar to a chocolate brownie mix, this rich chocolate cake also happens to be gluten-free, and is a fantastic finale

Serves 12 • Ready in 1 hour

FOR THE CAKE:
* 200g (7oz) butter
* 200g (7oz) dark chocolate
* 1tbsp strong espresso coffee
* 6 eggs
* 250g (9oz) caster sugar
* 60g (2oz) cocoa powder, sifted, plus extra to dust

FOR THE BAILEYS CREAM:
* 200ml (7fl oz) double cream
* 1-2tbsp sifted icing sugar
* 4tbsp Baileys original liqueur

FOR THE SALTED ALMOND PRALINE:
* 50g (2oz) caster sugar
* 2tbsp chopped blanched almonds, toasted

You will need:
A small baking sheet lined with oiled foil
20cm (8in) spring-form cake tin, greased and lined with baking paper
Gold leaf, to decorate, optional

1 For the praline, gently heat the sugar in a saucepan, then, as it begins to melt, turn up the heat to medium, swirling the pan, until all the sugar has melted and turned golden. Pour onto the oiled foil, scatter over the nuts and a little sea salt, and leave to cool and set. Once cold, break into pieces and blend in a food processor until coarsely ground. Set aside.
2 For the cake, melt the butter and chocolate together in a heatproof bowl over a pan of gently simmering water. Once melted, mix well, add the coffee and set aside.
3 Separate the eggs into two large bowls. Add the sugar to the yolks and whisk with an electric whisk until thick and pale. Whisk the egg whites to soft peaks. Add the cocoa and chocolate mixture to the egg yolks and whisk gently to combine, then stir in a third of the egg whites and fold the rest in.
4 Heat the air fryer to 150°C/275°F. Spoon the cake mixture into the tin and bake in the air fryer for 30 mins. Cool in the tin on a wire rack.
5 For the Baileys cream, use an electric whisk to whip the cream and icing sugar until firm, then slowly whisk in the liqueur. Dust the cake with cocoa powder, and serve in wedges with the Baileys cream, praline and a little gold leaf, if desired.

"The texture of the
cake is fudge-like.
A skewer inserted
into the centre should
come out piping hot
and clean"

New York Baked Cheesecake

Tangy lemon curd adds a mouth-watering tartness that cuts through the richness of this creamy cheesecake, with the pineapple flowers turning this all-time classic into a special-occasion bake. Make it a few days ahead and store in the fridge, but add the flowers to serve

Serves 8-10 * Ready in 1 hour 45 minutes, plus cooling and making the pineapple flowers

* 1 small, unripe pineapple, peeled and eyes removed
* 100g (3½oz) butter
* 250g (9oz) Ginger Nuts biscuits, whizzed to fine crumbs
* 500g (1lb) full-fat cream cheese, at room temperature
* 150g (5oz) caster sugar
* 3 eggs, well beaten
* 200g (7oz) soured cream
* 1tsp vanilla bean paste
* 20g (¾oz) cornflour
* 4tbsp lemon curd

You will need:
20cm (8in) round spring-clip tin, greased and base lined with baking paper; 12-hole muffin tin

1 A day or two before, make the pineapple flowers (see below).
2 For the cheesecake, melt the butter and mix in the biscuit crumbs. Press into the base of the round tin and push 4cm (1½in) up the edge of the tin, smoothing with the back of a spoon. Heat the air fryer to 160°C/300°F and bake the crust for 8-10 mins. Set aside to cool. Set the air fryer to 110°C/175°F.
3 In an electric stand mixer, whisk the cream cheese and sugar until smooth. Add the eggs, cream and vanilla. Sift over the cornflour and mix until smooth, then pour over the biscuit base. Tap the tray on the worktop to remove any air bubbles, and bake for 1 hr 10 mins.

4 Run a flat-bladed knife around the outside edge of the cheesecake to prevent cracking, then pull out the air fryer basket slightly and leave the cheesecake in the air fryer for an hr. Remove and cool completely on a wire rack.

5 Spread the lemon curd on top of the cheesecake, then chill for a couple of hrs before running a knife around the edge of the tin and transferring the cheesecake to a serving plate. Decorate with the pineapple flowers.

TO MAKE THE PINEAPPLE FLOWERS:
The day before, make the pineapple flowers. Cut **12** rounds of pineapple as thinly as possible; use a mandoline if you have one. Blot with kitchen towel to dry the fruit as much as possible, then lay on parchment liners. Heat the air fryer to 90°C/194°F. Bake the pineapple for 2 hrs 30 mins - 3 hrs. Every 30 mins peel off the paper and reorder the pineapple slices so they cook evenly. When they are dry, but still malleable, shape by pressing into a muffin tin or wine glasses and allow to cool. Store in an air tight container.

Almond-Topped Mince Pies

We love this alternative nutty mince pie topping. Silicone muffin cases are a great option to cupcake trays, most of which are too big to fit an air fryer. You'll need to bake them in two batches

Makes 12 * **Ready in 35 minutes**

* 325g (11oz) ready-rolled shortcrust pastry
* 300g (10oz) mincemeat

FOR THE ALMOND TOPPING:
* 3 egg whites
* 200g (7oz) icing sugar
* 200g (7oz) ground almonds
* 2tbsp flaked almonds

You will need:
12 silicone muffin cases

1 For the almond top, whisk the egg whites until stiff. Fold in the ground almonds. Unravel the pastry and cut out 12 rounds and line the cases. Spoon 1tbsp of mincemeat into each. Heat the air fryer to 150°C/275°F.
2 Spread over the topping and press three flaked almonds on top of each.
3 Cook for 15 mins until golden on top, carefully remove from the cases and bake for a further 5 mins to crisp up the bases. Cool on a wire rack.

Gingerbread House

Such a cute decoration for your Christmas cake, which the kids will love!

Ready in 20 minutes, plus chilling and cooling

* 30g (1oz) butter, softened
* 2tbsp light brown sugar
* 1tsp each ground cinnamon and ginger
* ½tsp mixed spice
* Zest of ½ orange
* 1tbsp golden syrup
* 1tbsp water
* 110g (4oz) plain flour
* Royal icing, to decorate (see Christmas cake recipe page 105)

You will need:
Ruler
Small star cutter
Piping bag fitted with a small, round nozzle
Small battery-powered lights

1 Combine the ingredients listed up to the royal icing, in a food processor. Blitz until the mixture comes together to form a dough. Wrap in cling film, then chill for 30 mins.
2 Roll out the dough to 3mm (just under ¼in) thick. Cut out two 12 x 10½cm (5 x 4½in) rectangles and punch out star shapes. Roll the leftover dough back together and cut two 8 x 10 x 10cm (3 x 4 x 4in) triangles. Cut a door and a star in one triangle. Heat the air fryer to 170°C/325°F. Bake for 10

mins, allow to cool. Roll the remaining dough into small balls and bake for 8-10 mins, then allow to cool.
3 Mix a little water with the royal icing to make it the consistency of treacle, then transfer to the piping bag. Pipe your decoration onto the biscuits. Return to the

switched-off (but still warm) air fryer for 3-5 mins. Transfer to a wire rack to cool.
4 Build the house out of the biscuits, securing with the icing. Allow the icing to set firm for a few hrs, then nestle lights inside and place on top of the Christmas cake.

Salted Caramel Pretzel Brownie Bites

Caramel, salt and chocolate are a perfect combination, and these are so quick to bake in the air fryer

Makes 14 * Ready in 30 minutes

* 75g (3oz) unsalted butter, plus extra for greasing
* 125g (4oz) dark chocolate, broken into pieces
* 1tsp instant coffee
* ½tsp sea salt flakes
* 2 eggs
* 125g (4oz) golden caster sugar
* 2tbsp plain flour
* 2tsp cocoa powder
* 2tbsp salted caramel spread
* 12 (around 30g/1oz) salted pretzels

You will need:
15x15cm (6x6in) square baking tin, greased and lined with parchment

1 Melt the butter and chocolate in a bowl set over a pan of simmering water. Add the coffee and ½tsp sea salt.

2 Whisk the eggs and sugar together until thick and pale. Fold in the melted chocolate mixture. Sift the flour and cocoa together and fold into the mixture. Heat the air fryer to 180°C/350°F.

3 Put the mixture into the tin, then drizzle over the caramel and use a butter knife to push it through the mixture to create a marbled effect. Tap the tin on the work surface. Place the pretzels on top. Bake for 15 mins – the brownies will be gooey in the middle but the top should look shiny and cracked when cooked. Allow to cool in the tin. Sprinkle over ½tsp sea salt flakes. Once cool, cut into squares.

Ginger and Chocolate Profiterole Wreath

It's fiddly and pretty much impossible to pipe choux pastry in to an air fryer, but we've found the perfect solution! Open freeze the raw pastry, then bag it up and bake from frozen in batches, for a light and speedy result

Makes 36 * Ready in 50 minutes

* 50g (2oz) unsalted butter
* 150ml (5fl oz) whole milk
* 4 balls of stem ginger in syrup, cut into quarters
* ½tsp sea salt
* 75g (3oz) plain flour
* 2 eggs, beaten

FOR THE FILLING:
* Finely grated zest of 1 orange
* 300ml (10fl oz) double cream

FOR THE GLAZE:
* 100g (3½oz) dark chocolate
* 2tsp golden syrup
* 1tbsp toasted chopped hazelnuts hazelnuts

1 In a pan, melt the butter. Add the milk, ginger and sea salt, and bring to the boil. Remove the ginger pieces and set aside until you are ready to make the filling. Take the boiling liquid off the heat, add the flour to the pan in one go and mix until it's a thick lump. Keep stirring until you have a smooth ball which leaves the sides of the pan. Slowly add the beaten eggs, using an electric hand whisk.

2 Pipe or spoon walnut-sized balls on to baking sheets lined with parchment. Open freeze, then once hard, bag them up until you are ready to bake.

3 When you are ready to assemble the wreath, heat the air fryer to 180°C/350°F. Bake the choux buns in batches for 10 mins, and cool on a wire rack. For the filling, blitz the ginger, orange zest and cream in a food processor until firm. Halve the buns and spoon in the filling.

4 For the glaze, melt the chocolate, syrup and 65ml (2½fl oz) water in a bowl set over a pan of simmering water. Mix until smooth and spoon over the buns and top with a scattering of hazelnuts.

Mini Panettone - Three Ways

Classic Panettone

We've found the best way to bake Italian panettone in an air fryer is to use silicone muffin cases, which you can cut with scissors, if necessary, to fit. You'll need to bake two batches

Makes 10 * **Ready in 30 minutes, plus rising**

* 500g (1lb) strong plain white flour
* 1tbsp fast-action yeast
* ½tsp vanilla bean paste
* 100g (3½oz) golden caster sugar
* 3 eggs
* 150ml (5fl oz) milk
* 125g (4oz) unsalted butter, melted
* 100g (3½oz) ricotta cheese
* 75g (3oz) mixed dried fruit
* 75g (3oz) pine nuts
* Finely grated zest of 1 lemon
* 2tbsp pearl sugar

TO FINISH:
1tbsp runny honey, optional

You will need:
10 silicone muffin cases
10 tulip muffin liners

1 Combine the plain white flour, a pinch of salt, fast-action yeast, vanilla bean paste and golden caster sugar together in a large bowl of a mixer fitted with a dough hook. Make a well in the centre and add the eggs, milk and melted butter once cooled.
2 In another bowl, mix together the ricotta, dried fruit, pine nuts and lemon zest. Tip into the bowl with the flour and eggs.
3 Turn on the mixer and combine ingredients together. Mix for several mins in the machine, or about 10 mins by hand, to make a very sticky dough. Cover and leave in a warm place, for about 1½ hrs to rise, or until it has doubled in size.
4 Heat the air fryer to 180°C/350°F. Line the silicone muffin cases with tulip muffin liners. Use an ice-cream scoop to divide the mixture between them. Sprinkle on the pearl sugar.
5 Bake for 15 mins, until golden brown. Tap the bases – if they sound hollow they're ready. Glaze with honey, if using.

Mango and Chocolate Panettone

Use the plain recipe, but omit the dried fruit, pine nuts and lemon zest, and replace with these ingredients:

* 75g (3oz) dried mango, chopped
* 75g (3oz) dark chocolate, chopped
* Finely grated zest of 1 orange

TO FINISH:
* 200g (7oz) dark chocolate
* 2tsp vegetable oil
* Dried mango strips, optional
* Ribbon and artificial berries

1 Put the chocolate and oil in a bowl, resting over a pan of simmering water and heat to melt.
2 Spoon the chocolate over the top of each mini panettone and arrange a dried mango strip on top, if you like.
3 Decorate with a ribbon and berries.

White Chocolate and Cranberry Panettone

Use the plain recipe, but omit the dried fruit and pine nuts. Replace with the following ingredients:

* 75g (3oz) dried cranberries
* 75g (3oz) white chocolate, chopped

TO FINISH:

* 200g (7oz) bar white chocolate, broken into squares
* 2tsp vegetable oil
* Mini snowflake sprinkles
* Decorative string
* Mini candy cane

1 To finish off, put the chocolate and oil in a bowl, resting over a pan of simmering water and heat to melt.
2 Spoon the chocolate over the top of each mini panettone and scatter over a few mini snowflake sprinkles.
3 Decorate by tying around the string and adding a mini candy cane.

Cook's tip

These panettone are best made and eaten within 2 days. Or prepare ahead and freeze for up to 1 month. Gently warm through to freshen up.

125

Mincemeat Soufflés

Soufflés work well in an air fryer, but they do tend to brown a little more than in the oven – nothing a dusting of icing sugar can't fix!

Serves 4 * Ready in 20 minutes

* 150g (5oz) mincemeat
* 1tbsp cornflour, mixed with 2tbsp water to make a smooth paste
* 150g (5oz) egg white (about 4 egg whites)
* 4tbsp caster sugar
* 4 Kirsch cherries
* 1tbsp flaked almonds, toasted
* Icing sugar, to serve

You will need:
4 ramekins, brushed lightly with melted butter and chilled

1 Heat the mincemeat with 1tbsp water and the cornflour paste. Bring to a boil to thicken, then allow to cool. Whisk the egg white until no longer yellow.

2 Gradually add the sugar until the whisk leaves a trail in the mix and the texture resembles shaving foam.

3 Beat a third of the meringue mixture into the mincemeat. Then fold in the rest of the meringue, a third at a time, until fully combined. Don't overdo it, as you don't want to knock all the air out of the mixture. Put a few dollops of the mixture into each ramekin. Using a palette knife, carefully make sure the mixture comes right up the sides but leave a small dip in the middle for a cherry.

4 Place a cherry inside each and cover the hole with more meringue mix. Use the palette knife to scrape off the excess mixture so it's all on top. Run a small knife around the edge of the ramekin, as this will help your soufflés to rise. Heat the air fryer to 190°C/375°F.

5 Bake for 10 mins. Top with the almonds and some sifted icing sugar and serve immediately.

> **"Add a spoonful of chocolate chips to your soufflés for a surprise treat"**

Gingerbread Flapjacks

These keep for up to three days in an airtight tin, so are perfect snacking material

Makes 16   Ready in 30 minutes

* 200g (7oz) unsalted butter, plus extra for greasing
* 75g (3oz) caster sugar
* 100g (3½oz) golden syrup
* 50g (2oz) black treacle
* 2tsps ground ginger
* 20g (¾oz) crystallised ginger, finely chopped, plus extra to decorate
* 450g (1lb) porridge oats
* 100g (3½oz) raisins
* 200g (7oz) white chocolate, broken up
* Soft gold edible pearls, to decorate

You will need:
* Two 15 x 15cm (6 x 6in) square tins, or similar. Make two batches

1 Put the butter, sugar, syrup, treacle and both gingers in a pan and heat gently to melt the butter. Remove from the heat and stir in the oats and raisins. Mix well and spoon into the tins, pressing down gently with the back of a damp spoon.
2 Heat the air fryer to 180°C/ 350°F. Cover the tin tightly with foil. Bake for 12-15 mins, then uncover and bake for 3-4 mins or until just starting to look cooked around the edges. The flapjack will still look soft in the centre. Leave in the tin to cool.
3 Melt the chocolate, either in a heatproof bowl resting over (not in) a pan of hot water or in short bursts In the microwave. Remove the cold flapjack from the tin and spread with the chocolate. Sprinkle with extra crystallised ginger and gold pearls. Leave to set before cutting into squares.

Snowy Black Forest Gâteau

Black Forest flavours are making a big comeback. And once you've tasted this combination of rich chocolate, booze-soaked cherries and indulgent creamy icing, you'll see why

Serves 12 * Ready in 1 hour, plus decorating

* 370g (13oz) jar cherries in kirsch, drained, Kirsch reserved

FOR THE CHOCOLATE SPONGE:
* 175g (6oz) unsalted butter, softened
* 200g (7oz) golden caster sugar
* 3 free-range eggs
* 1tsp vanilla bean paste
* 100g (3½oz) dark chocolate, melted
* 200g (7oz) self-raising flour
* 2tbsp cocoa powder
* ½tsp bicarbonate of soda
* 150g (5oz) soured cream

FOR THE MASCARPONE ICING:
* 300g (10oz) white chocolate
* 300g (10oz) mascarpone cheese
* 150g (5oz) double cream

FOR THE CHOCOLATE CURLS:
* 100g (3½oz) white chocolate, melted

You will need:
2 x 18cm (7in) loose-bottomed cake tins, lined with baking parchment

1 Using an electric mixer, for the sponge, beat the butter with the caster sugar until pale and creamy. Beat in the eggs, one at a time, then add the vanilla, melted chocolate (allow to cool for 5 mins), flour, cocoa powder and bicarbonate of soda, mixing until combined. Fold in the soured cream. Divide the mixture between the prepared tins, level the tops. Cover with foil, secure with string if necessary, then make a few holes in the top with a metal skewer. Heat the air fryer to 160°C/300°F. Bake, one tin at a time, for 20 mins, then remove the foil and bake for a further 10 mins. Leave to cool in the tins.

2 For the mascarpone icing, melt the white chocolate in a bowl set over a pan of boiling water (don't let the water touch the bowl). In a mixing bowl, beat together the mascarpone and cream, then fold into the melted white chocolate.

3 Put one of the sponges on a cake stand or plate and drizzle with 2tbsp of the kirsch from the cherry jar. Spread over some cream mixture, then scatter with half of the drained cherries. Sandwich the second sponge on top, and use a palette knife to cover the top and sides of the cake with the icing.

4 Meanwhile, put the remaining kirsch in a small pan and simmer over a medium heat until the liquid is reduced, and thick and syrupy. Set aside to cool.

5 For the chocolate curls, melt the white chocolate and spread onto the underside of two greased baking trays. Leave to set, then drag a cheese plane over the surface to create curls. Chill in a sealed container until needed.

6 Arrange the remaining cherries on top of the cake, drizzle with the cooled syrup and arrange the chocolate curls on top.

Lebkuchen Cookies

A traditional German biscuit that's synonymous with glittering Christmas markets. You will need to bake these in batches

Makes 24 * Ready in 30 minutes, plus chilling and cooling

* 100g (3½oz) honey
* 100g (3½oz) muscovado sugar
* 90g (3oz) unsalted butter
* 250g (9oz) self-raising flour
* 1tsp baking powder
* 1tbsp ground ginger
* 1tsp ground cinnamon
* ½tsp mixed spice
* ¼tsp ground nutmeg
* 100g (3½oz) ground almonds
* Zest of 1 orange
* 100g (3½oz) icing sugar
* 1-2tbsp water or orange juice

You will need:
Parchment air fryer liners with holes punched in (buy these pre-done) or a silicone liner

1 In a small pan, melt the honey, muscovado and butter together. Set aside. In a bowl, sift together the flour, baking powder, and spices, along with the ground almonds. Add the zest of the orange, pour over the butter mixture and mix into a dough. Wrap in baking paper and chill for 15-20 mins.

2 Heat the air fryer to 180°C/350°F. On a floured surface, roll the dough to 1cm (½in) thick and cut desired shapes. Place on parchment liners and bake in batches for 8-10 mins – these should still be soft when baked. Remove from the air fryer and leave to cool on a wire rack.

3 Meanwhile, mix the icing sugar and liquid together until smooth, dip the top of the biscuits in the glaze and leave to set. If you desire, melt some dark chocolate and coat the bottom and/or decorate on top. Leave to set.

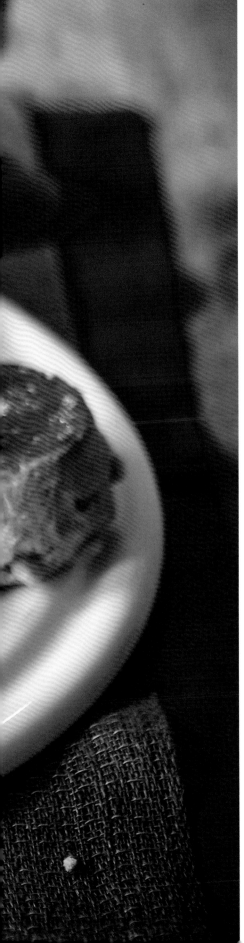

Festive Scones with Spiced Cherry Jam

Homemade scones, jam and boozy butter – these will really impress your loved ones! Ideally, make the jam the day before

Serves 20 * **Ready in 1 hour, plus cooling**

* 500g (1lb 2oz) plain flour
* 2tbsp baking powder
* 90g (3oz) caster sugar
* 125g (4oz) unsalted butter, cold and cubed
* 200g (7oz) candied peel
* 2-3 pieces of stem ginger, chopped
* Zest of 1 orange
* 2 eggs, plus 1 yolk for the egg wash
* 150ml (5fl oz) buttermilk

FOR THE SPICED CHERRY JAM:
* 250g (9oz) frozen cherries
* 125g (4oz) cherries in syrup, drained and rinsed
* Juice of 1 lemon
* 150g (5oz) jam sugar
* 1tbsp cinnamon

FOR THE AMARETTO BUTTER:
* 125g (4oz) unsalted butter, softened
* 1tsp vanilla paste
* 3tbsp Amaretto

You will need:
6cm (2½in) round cutter; sterilised, airtight jam jar Pierced parchment air fryer liners

1 For the scones, sift the flour, baking powder, caster sugar and a pinch of salt together in a large bowl, then rub in the butter until it resembles breadcrumbs. Add in the candied peel, stem ginger and orange zest. Add the eggs and buttermilk, and mix into a dough. Turn out on to a lightly floured surface and knead lightly into a ball. Heat the air fryer to 180°C/350°F.
2 Roll out to 2½cm (1in) and cut out the scones with the round cutter. Place on the liners, brush with the egg yolk and bake in batches for 8 mins, turning halfway through, until golden brown.
3 Meanwhile, for the spiced cherry jam, add all the ingredients to a large pan and cook over a high heat until boiling and the fruit has started to break down, which should be around 10-15 mins. Leave to cool slightly before transferring to the sterilised jar.
4 For the Amaretto butter, use a stand mixer or a handheld electric whisk to whip the butter until light, pale and fluffy. Add the vanilla paste and Amaretto, 1tbsp at a time, while still whipping, until it is all incorporated.
5 Serve the scones warm with a spread of the spiced cherry jam, and a dollop of the whipped Amaretto butter.

Cook's tip

Scones freeze extremely well. Just reheat for 2-3 mins in the air fryer.

IN-BETWEEN

**PERFECT DISHES FOR THE PERIOD
BETWEEN CHRISTMAS AND NEW YEAR**

Ultimate Leftovers Toastie

Breathe new life into the tasty odds and ends lingering in the fridge. You can use up almost anything in this moreish snack!

Serves 2 • Ready in 15 minutes

- 2 large slices sourdough bread
- 65g (2½oz) leftover cheese, grated or crumbled
- 1 egg
- ½tsp Worcestershire sauce
- 1tsp milk
- 1 spring onion, finely chopped
- 1tsp fresh herbs, finely chopped
- Splash wine or beer, optional
- 1-2tsp cranberry sauce
- 1tbsp mayonnaise
- ½tbsp grainy mustard
- 30g (1oz) leftover meat: ham, turkey, stuffing or pigs in blankets
- Gravy, for dipping, optional

1 Heat the air fryer to 180°C/350°F. Toast the bread for 2 mins a side in the air fryer.

2 In a bowl, combine the cheese, egg, Worcestershire sauce, milk, spring onion, herbs (we used thyme and rosemary) and a splash of wine or beer if you have some open.

3 Spread one slice of toast with cranberry sauce, then divide the cheese mixture between the 2 toasts and bake in the air fryer on a silicone mat for 6 mins, until hot and bubbling.

4 Mix the mayonnaise and mustard. Top the cranberry/cheese toast with the leftover meat stuffing, add the mustard mayo, then sandwich with the second toast, cheese side up. Serve with warm gravy to dip.

"For a veggie option, use nut roast and vegan cheese"

Duck Fat Chips with Thyme and Oregano Salt

An air fryer can produce fabulous chips with much less fat. Most air fryers have a pre-set programme for chips, or follow our guidelines. These are so tasty – perfect with a juicy steak

Serves 2-3 * **Ready in 35 minutes, plus soaking**

* 4 large baking potatoes, peeled
* 2tbsp duck or goose fat, melted
* 4 sprigs fresh thyme
* 1tbsp sea salt
* 2tsp chopped fresh thyme
* 1tsp dried oregano
* Crushed black pepper

1 Cut the potatoes into 1cm (½in) chips, as evenly as you can. Immerse them in a bowl of cold water and leave in the fridge for 30 mins. This draws out the starch and makes for a crisper chip. Heat the air fryer to 180°C/350°F (or use the pre-set). Drain and dry well on a clean tea towel. Toss them in the melted duck fat.
2 Tip them in a single layer into the air fryer (you may need two batches) and fry for 15 mins, shaking once. If they aren't browned enough, increase the temperature to 200°C/400°F and cook for a further 5 mins.
3 Transfer to serving bowls, mix the herbs with the salt then scatter over the chips.

Turkey Enchiladas

Put a Mexican twist on turkey with these deliciously easy enchiladas packed full of flavour and colour

Serves 4 · **Ready in 35 minutes**

- 2tbsp olive oil
- 1 red onion, chopped
- 1 red pepper, sliced
- 1 yellow pepper, chopped
- 250g (9oz) cooked turkey/ chicken, shredded
- 1-2tbsp ready-made fajita seasoning
- 200g (7oz) tin chopped tomatoes/passata
- 250g (9oz) tomato salsa
- Handful fresh coriander, chopped, plus extra leaves to garnish
- 6 small tortilla wraps
- 125g (4oz) crème fraîche or soured cream
- 100g (3½oz) Cheddar, coarsely grated
- 1 green chilli, sliced, optional

- Lime wedges, to serve
- Mashed avocado

1 Heat the oil in a large frying pan, then fry the onion and peppers for 10 mins over a medium-high heat, until softened and browned.

2 Add the turkey or chicken and stir-fry, then add the spice mix and cook for a few mins. Stir in the tomatoes and half the salsa, then simmer for 15 mins until cooked through. Stir in most of the coriander.

3 Heat the air fryer to 180°C/350°F. Divide the mixture between 6 wraps, rolling each as you go, and put in a medium dish which fits your air fryer (you may need to cook in two batches). Spoon over the crème fraîche or soured cream, then scatter over the cheese. Bake for 10 mins. Serve with coriander, chilli, lime wedges, salsa and avocado, as wished.

Turkey and Parsnip One-pot Pie

This hearty pie works perfectly
with leftover turkey or chicken

Serves 4 * **Ready in
1 hour 25 minutes**

- 1 sheet ready-rolled puff pastry
- 100g (3½oz) diced pancetta
  or lardons
- 1 large leek, finely sliced
- ½ savoy cabbage, shredded
- 1tbsp cornflour
- 1tbsp Dijon mustard with herbs
- 200ml (7fl oz) dry white wine
- 200g (7oz) button
  mushrooms, halved
- 3 parsnips, peeled and chopped
  into chunks
- 400g (14oz) cooked turkey, cut
  into bite-sized pieces
- 1 egg, beaten

You will need:
- 18-20cm (7-8in) heatproof round
  casserole dish which fits in your
  air fryer

1 Cut a disc of pastry the size of
the casserole dish, then put the
cut pastry in the fridge. You
could use the leftovers to cut out
shapes to decorate the top of
the pie.
2 In the casserole dish, cook the
pancetta until golden. Remove
the meat, leaving the fat in the
pan. Add the leek. Sweat with
the lid on, over a low heat, for
about 10 mins, stirring
occasionally, until softened. Mix
in the cabbage and cornflour,
return the lid and sweat for 10

mins, removing the lid after 5
mins. Add the mustard and wine,
and season. Scrape the brown
bits from the base of the pan and
simmer for 10 mins.
3 Mix in the mushrooms,
parsnips and turkey, season and
return the pancetta to the pan.
Cover with the pastry and make
a small incision in the centre. If
using, lay over the cut-out pastry
shapes and brush the top with
the beaten egg. Chill for 15 min.
Heat the air fryer to 190°C/375°F.
4 Bake in air fryer for 15-20 mins
until the pastry is golden and the
filling is piping hot.

Creamy Sprout and Potato Gratin

This rich side dish is a real treat, and is a perfect one to prepare ahead

Serves 4 • Ready in 45 minutes

- 300g (10oz) baking potatoes, peeled and cut into chunks
- 300g (10oz) small Brussels sprouts, trimmed and halved
- 1 onion, diced
- ½tbsp olive oil
- 90g (3oz) smoked bacon lardons
- 4tbsp white wine
- 250g (9oz) crème fraîche
- 100g (3½oz) Reblochon, Tallegio or other soft melting cheese, cut into 2cm (¾in) chunks
- 2tbsp breadcrumbs

1 Put the potatoes into a large pan, cover with cold water, add a good pinch of sea salt, bring to a boil and cook for 7 mins. Add the sprouts and cook for 3 mins more, then drain.
2 Meanwhile, in a large frying pan over a medium heat, fry the onion in the oil until turning golden. Set aside. Increase the heat and fry the lardons, mixing until golden. Add the onions. Deglaze the pan with the wine and bring to a boil to reduce. Off the heat, stir in the crème fraîche, ½tsp sea salt, the sprouts and potatoes. Then transfer to a round 18-20cm (7-8in) ovenproof dish. Arrange the cheese on top, then press in the breadcrumbs.
3 Heat the air fryer to 160°C/300°F and bake the gratin for 15 mins.

Cook's tip
You can also fry the lardons in the air fryer at 200°C/400°F for 8 mins in a silicone liner (we like the ones with sides, like a cake tin liner – less mess!). Toss halfway through cooking.

"For vegans, use
dairy-free butter
for brushing the
filo pastry"

Veggie Filo Quiche

Using filo instead of shortcrust pastry means this quiche is super light

Serves 4 • Ready in 25 minutes

* 4 large sheets filo pastry
* 50g (1¾oz) butter, melted
* 125g (4oz) bag baby-leaf spinach
* 4 eggs, whisked
* 3tbsp semi-skimmed milk
* Small bunch of mint, chopped
* 100g (3½oz) marinated artichoke hearts, halved
* 100g (3½oz) feta cheese, crumbled
* Salad leaves, to serve

1 Line a loose-bottomed 18-20cm (7-8in) tart case with the filo sheets, leaving some overhang. Brush each layer of pastry with melted butter, then fold the overhang back into the case and brush with more butter.
2 Prick the spinach bag with a fork and microwave for 30 secs, until the leaves are just softened. Open the bag carefully and allow to cool slightly before handling. Squeeze out any excess water.
3 Heat the air fryer to 180°C/350°F. Put the eggs, milk and mint into a large bowl, season with salt and freshly ground black pepper and whisk until combined. Arrange the spinach, artichoke hearts and feta in the filo case and pour over the egg mix. Air fry for 15 mins. Serve hot or cold with a crisp green salad.

Fried Chicken Salad Platter

An air fryer makes the best fried chicken ever, without the fat, faff and frying!

Serves 4 · **Ready in 25 minutes, plus marinating**

- 8 chicken pieces with skin on
- 500ml (16fl oz) buttermilk
- 3tbsp self-raising flour
- 3tbsp rice flour
- 2tsp garlic salt
- 1¼tsp ground white pepper
- 1½tbsp sweet smoked paprika
- Good pinch chilli flakes
- ½tsp Chinese 5 spice
- 1tsp dried oregano
- 1tsp dried thyme
- 450g (1lb) baby vine tomatoes
- 1tbsp oil
- ½tbsp cider vinegar
- ¾tsp Dijon mustard
- ¾tsp runny honey
- 3 little gem lettuces, torn
- Handful watercress leaves

1 Mix the chicken with almost all the buttermilk – reserve 75ml (3fl oz) for the dressing. Chill for 4 hrs or overnight. Remove the chicken from the fridge. Heat the air fryer to 200°C/400°F.

2 Mix the flours, garlic salt, pepper, spices and dried herbs together. Remove the chicken from the buttermilk, pat dry and toss in the spice mix. Air fry for 15 mins, flip and cook for a further 6 mins.
You may need to do two batches. Remove the chicken. Toss the tomatoes in oil and air fry for 3 mins in a parchment liner with sides or shallow dish.

3 Mix the vinegar, mustard and honey with reserved buttermilk; season. Spread the salad leaves in a dish, top with chicken and tomatoes, and drizzle over the dressing.

Curried Veggie Samosa Pasties

Curried potatoes and root veg work a treat with spices. For extra oomph, add a sliced green chilli and 2tsp chaat masala. The pastry is worth the extra effort, but swap for bought shortcrust if you're short on time

Makes 4 * Ready in 50 minutes, plus chilling

FOR THE PASTRY:
* 300g (10oz) plain flour, plus extra to dust
* 200g (7oz) cold unsalted butter, cubed
* 2tbsp nigella (kalonji) seeds
* 1 egg, lightly beaten
* 3tbsp milk
* 2tsp white wine vinegar
* 1 egg, beaten, to glaze

FOR THE FILLING:
* 400g (14oz) leftover roasted veg, cut into 2cm (¾in) chunks, we used potatoes, carrots and parsnips
* 200g (7oz) spinach, blanched
* 1tsp coriander seeds, toasted and ground
* 1tsp fennel seeds, toasted and ground
* 1tsp ground cumin
* 2tbsp lime pickle
* Handful coriander, roughly chopped
* Juice 1 lime

1 In a food processor, whizz up the flour and butter with 1tsp sea salt until fine crumbs. Add the nigella seeds, egg, milk and vinegar. Whizz until a soft dough. Shape the dough into a ball, flatten into a disc, cover in cling film and chill for 30 mins.

2 In a large bowl, combine all the filling ingredients.
3 Divide the pastry into 4 equal pieces. Roll out one piece on a lightly floured surface to form a circle roughly 5mm (¼in) thick.
4 Pile a quarter of the filling onto one half of the pastry, leaving a 3cm (1¼in) border. Brush the edges with a little beaten egg, then fold the other half over and press to enclose the filling. Crimp the edge and place on a large, lined baking sheet.

5 Repeat with the remaining pastry and filling. Brush the pasties with the egg wash, chill for 20 mins then egg wash again. Heat the air fryer to 180°C/350°F. Bake the pastries for 10 mins, then flip, glaze again then bake for a further 10 mins until golden brown and heated through (you may need to do two batches, depending on the size of your air fryer).
6 Serve with chutney or raita on the side.

Lamb Fillet with Celeriac Purée and Tapenade Dressing

An elegant, yet quick and easy dinner for two. The lamb should be medium rare for the best flavour, otherwise it may dry out too much and become chewy

Serves 2 • Ready in 25 minutes

- 350g (12oz) piece lamb fillet
- 1tsp olive oil
- 1tsp thyme leaves
- 250g (9oz) celeriac, diced
- 250ml (9fl oz) whole milk
- 1 garlic clove, lightly bruised
- 13tbsp black olive tapenade
- 3tbsp virgin olive oil
- 2tbsp capers, drained
- 1tsp pink peppercorns, lightly crushed

1 Place the lamb in a shallow glass dish with the oil, add the thyme leaves and season with ground black pepper and salt. Leave, covered, to marinate until you're ready to cook.
2 Put the celeriac in a pan with the milk and bruised garlic clove. Bring to a simmer and cook for 8-10 mins, until tender. Drain, reserving the cooking liquid, and remove the garlic clove. Using a hand blender, whizz the celeriac until smooth, loosening with cooking liquid if needed. Season to taste and keep warm.
3 Heat the air fryer to 200°C/400°F. Cook the lamb for 6 mins, turning halfway through, until browned on the outside. Remove and rest for 5 mins.
4 Meanwhile, make the dressing by whisking together the tapenade and virgin olive oil. Stir through the capers.
5 To serve, spoon a layer of celeriac purée on to a platter, top with the sliced lamb and drizzle over some tapenade dressing and sprinkle over pink peppercorns.

Cook's tip
You can leave the beef tightly wrapped in cling film for up to 2 days in the fridge. It also makes slicing easier.

Rare Asian-Style Beef with Chilli Salad and Dipping Sauce

Topside of beef represents great value for money, but you do need to eat it rare or just over or it will be tough. Leftovers are great for roast beef sandwiches too

Serves 8-12 · Ready in 1 hour 15 minutes, plus cooling

- A little oil
- 1¾kg (2lb 12oz) beef topside
- 2tbsp Sichuan pepper

FOR THE DIPPING SAUCE:
- 2tbsp soy sauce
- Juice of 1 lime
- ¼tsp Sichuan pepper
- 1tbsp palm sugar
- 2tbsp rice vinegar

FOR THE SALAD:
- 2 red chillies, sliced lengthways
- 5tbsp chopped fresh coriander
- 10 spring onions, sliced on the diagonal
- 2 carrots, julienned
- 2tbsp rice vinegar
- 1tbsp sesame oil

1 Heat the air fryer to 200°C/400°F. Rub a little oil all over the beef. Roast for 30 min, then reduce the heat to 150°C/275°F. It should be rare but not raw in the middle, so the internal temperature with a meat thermometer should be 45°C/125°F – it will cook further on resting. Rub in the pepper. Leave it to cool completely.
2 Mix the ingredients together for both the dipping sauce and the salad. Thinly slice the beef and arrange on a board or platter.

Cheese and Chive Soda Bread

Soda bread is simple to make, with no proving or rising time needed. It's best eaten on the day, but any leftovers make great toast

Serves 4-6 · Ready in 45 minutes

- 200g (7oz) natural yoghurt
- 75ml (3oz) Guinness or another stout
- 225g (8oz) plain flour
- 100g (3½oz) plain wholemeal flour
- ¼tsp sea salt
- 1tsp bicarbonate of soda
- 1tbsp pumpkin seeds, plus extra for the top
- A handful of chives, snipped into cm lengths
- 60g (2oz) leftover cheese, grated or crumbled

1 In a jug combine the yoghurt and stout. Put the flours, salt, bicarbonate of soda, seeds, chives and three quarters of the cheese in a bowl and add the yoghurt mixture. Mix until just combined. Don't worry about floury patches yet. Set aside for about 10 mins to make the dough more workable.

2 Heat the air fryer to 180°C/350°F. Knead the dough until smooth. Don't worry, it will be quite sticky. With floury hands shape the sticky dough into a ball and place onto a floured silicone liner. Flatten down the top to create a thick disc and sprinkle over the remaining cheese and seeds. Use the side of a floured wooden spoon to press a deep cross into the top of the loaf. Bake for 20 mins, then flip and bake for a further 10 mins. Transfer to a wire rack to cook.

Baked Fondue Cheese

Such a great sharing dish, perfect with pre-lunch or dinner drinks

Serves 4-6 * Ready in 20 minutes

* 200g (7oz) Brie or Camembert, rind removed
* 125g (4½oz) Gruyère cheese
* 100g (3½oz) cream cheese
* 3tbsp milk or white wine
* 2tbsp Parmesan cheese, grated
* 2tsp cornflour
* 5tbsp chutney
* 1tsp thyme sprigs
* Bread, to serve

1 Put the cheeses and cream cheese into a processor with milk or wine, half the Parmesan and cornflour. Blend until smooth.

Spoon the chutney into the base of a shallow ovenproof dish (or two smaller ones, whichever fit into your air fryer) and spoon on the creamy cheese. Season well, sprinkle with thyme and the remaining Parmesan.

2 Heat the air fryer to 160°C/300°F. Bake for 15 mins. Serve with large croutons or breadsticks.

Turkey, Ham and Chestnut Pie

Here's a satisfying way of using up festive leftovers

Serves 2-3 * **Ready in 1 hour, plus chilling**

* 30g (1oz) butter, plus extra for greasing
* 450g (1lb leeks), trimmed and cut into 1cm-thick (½in) slices
* 1tsp thyme leaves
* 2tbsp plain flour
* 250ml (9fl oz) turkey stock
* 150g (5oz) cooked turkey, cut into large pieces
* 100g (3½oz) cooked ham, cut into cubes
* 50g (2oz) cooked chestnuts, quartered
* 3tbsp crème fraîche
* Grating of fresh nutmeg
* 200g (7oz) ready-made puff pastry
* 1 egg yolk, beaten

You will need:
* 18-20cm (7-8in) pie dish

1 Melt the butter in a large pan, add the leeks and thyme, then stir, cover and cook gently for 15 mins until soft. Add the flour and stir well. Pour in the stock, stirring, until you have a smooth sauce. Add the meats, chestnuts and crème fraîche. Season with black pepper, nutmeg and salt. Stir well to combine.

2 Put the filling into the pie dish. Butter the rim of the dish. Roll the pastry out to the thickness of a £1 coin, cut several strips and press them around the edges of the dish. Brush with water and lie a pastry lid on top. Make 2 small steam holes.

3 Press the pastry edges together, trim off any excess, then crimp the edges. Use the excess pastry to decorate the top. Mix the egg yolk with 1tsp water and brush all over the pastry. Chill for 10 mins. Heat the air fryer to 190°C/375°F.

4 Bake for 15-20 mins, or until the pastry is brown and the filling piping hot. Serve immediately.

Cook's tip

It's quite tricky to get a runny tart into a hot fryer, so make a long sling or hammock with folded foil, then put it under the tin and use the foil "handles" to lower in the quiche.

Brie and Cranberry Quiche

Filling, gooey and simply delicious. Use shop-bought shortcrust pastry if you prefer. Check out our cook's tip on how to get a raw quiche into a hot air fryer without spillage!

Serves 6 · Ready in 1 hour, plus chilling

FOR THE PASTRY:
- 200g (7oz) plain flour
- 100g (3½oz) chilled butter, cubed
- 1 egg

FOR THE FILLING:
- 30g (1oz) butter
- 1 large onion, chopped
- 250g (9oz) streaky bacon, chopped
- 5 eggs, lightly beaten
- 250g (9oz) crème fraîche
- 125g (4oz) Brie, sliced
- 3tbsp cranberry sauce
- 60g (2½oz) Cheddar cheese, grated

You will need:
18-20cm (7-8in) loose-based tart tin, greased

1 For the pastry, put the flour, butter and a pinch of salt into a food processor. Whizz until the mixture resembles crumbs, then add the egg and 1tbsp cold water. Blend until just bound. Turn out onto a lightly floured work surface and knead until smooth. Wrap in cling film and chill for 30 mins.

2 Roll out the pastry and use to line the tin. Chill for 20 mins. Heat the air fryer to 180°C/350°F. Trim the pastry case and bake blind for 10 mins, then remove the paper and baking beans and cook for 5 mins more. Set aside.

3 Meanwhile, heat the butter and fry the onions gently for 5 mins to soften. Air fry the bacon in a parchment liner for 3-4 mins, shaking halfway, until crisp. Put on kitchen paper to drain.

4 Crack the eggs into a jug, add the crème fraîche, season and whisk. Spoon the onions and bacon into the pastry case. Arrange the Brie on top with teaspoonfuls of cranberry sauce. Scatter over the Cheddar, and pour egg mixture over. Air fry for 15 mins, then cover tightly with foil. Reduce the temperature to 160°C/300°F and bake for a further 25 mins. Serve warm.

Cheese and Pesto Sausage Rolls

This twist on the buffet classic is packed with flavour. For the air fryer, it's best to open-freeze them, bag up then bake from frozen as you need them

Makes 24 · **Ready in 30 minutes, plus freezing**

- 450g (1lb) free-range pork sausage meat
- 2-3tbsp Sacla' No 16 'Nduja Pesto or sun-dried tomato pesto
- 125g (4oz) mature Cheddar, grated
- 1 fresh rosemary sprig, leaves chopped
- 4 fresh thyme sprigs, leaves chopped
- 500g (1lb 1oz) puff pastry
- 1 medium free-range egg, beaten

1 In a mixing bowl, combine the sausage meat, 'nduja pesto, 3tbsp Cheddar, herbs, and salt and black pepper.
2 On a lightly floured surface, roll out the pastry lengthways to a rectangle 38 x 25cm (15 x 10in). Cut this in half lengthways, then place half the sausage mixture down the length of each half of the pastry, just off- centre, keeping it in a 2-3cm-wide (¾ - 1¼in) sausage shape. Lightly brush either exposed edge of the pastry with egg, then fold the wider edge over onto the other exposed edge to encase the meat. Press down along the lip to seal, then brush with egg to glaze.
3 Cut each long roll into 12 sausage rolls, and transfer to parchment-lined baking sheets to open freeze. Brush with a little extra egg to glaze, then freeze.
4 To cook, heat the air fryer to 200°C/400°F. Bake from frozen for 10-11 mins, or for 8 mins if not. Once cooked, sprinkle with Cheddar and leave in the switched off air fryer for a few mins to melt the cheese. (This stage is optional). Serve with chutney or tomato ketchup.

Giant Sausage Roll with Cheese and Pickle

A much-loved classic, this version benefits from the piquant tang of Branston inside!

Make 12 slices * Ready in 45 minutes

* 375g (13oz) puff pastry

FOR THE FILLING:
* 600g (1lb 4oz) pork sausage meat
* 3tbsp Branston Pickle
* 45g (1½oz) Cheddar cheese, grated
* 1 egg, beaten

1 Roll out the pastry to a 30 x 22cm (12 x 8½in) rectangle. Keep the trimmings for decoration. Chill the pastry while you make the filling.
2 Pat out half the sausage meat to 30cm (12in) in length on a piece of baking paper. This will make it easier to roll up.
3 Spoon the pickle over the centre of the sausage meat, then add a line of cheese through the centre. Pat over the rest of the sausage meat.
4 Use the baking paper to roll it into a long sausage shape, keeping the cheese and pickle in the middle as much as possible.
5 Brush the pastry edges with beaten egg then put the sausage meat in the centre and join the pastry around it. Cut in half so it fits the air fryer basket.
6 Flip over, brush with the egg, decorate with the pastry trimmings and glaze again. Heat the air fryer to 200°C/400°F. Bake for 12-15 mins until golden brown and cooked all the way through. Allow to cool slightly before serving.

Smoked Salmon and Potato Crustless Quiche

No faffing about with pastry here – just layer in a tin and bake. A simple dish, perfect for a holiday brunch

Serves 2-3 • Ready in 30 minutes

• 400g (14oz) new potatoes, cooked
• 100g (3½oz) smoked salmon
• 3 spring onions, sliced
• 1tbsp chopped fresh dill
• 4 eggs
• 2tbsp crème fraîche

You will need:
18cm (7in) round tin, with a parchment liner with edges

1 Slice the potatoes and arrange half of them over the base of the lined tin. Season with salt and pepper.
2 Arrange half the smoked salmon in strips over the potatoes and scatter over half of the spring onions and half of the dill. Repeat the layers with the remaining potatoes, salmon, spring onions and dill.
3 Heat the air fryer to 160°C/300°F. Beat together the eggs and crème fraîche and pour over the layered veg and salmon. Bake for 25 mins until browned and just set. It will carry on setting on cooling. Serve warm or at room temperature.

Duck and Healthy Greens Salad

Think Chinese-style crispy duck with a punchy Asian dressing served with crunchy greens

Serves 6 · Ready in 1 hour 45 minutes

FOR THE DUCK:
- 4 duck legs
- 150ml (5fl oz) soy sauce
- Small piece of root ginger, roughly chopped
- 4 garlic cloves, bruised
- 2 star anise
- 1 cinnamon stick

FOR THE SALAD:
- 300g (10oz) tenderstem broccoli
- 300g (10oz) kale, shredded
- 4tbsp mixed seeds, lightly toasted

FOR THE DRESSING:
- 2tbsp sweet miso paste
- 1tbsp toasted sesame oil
- Juice of 2 limes
- 1tbsp runny honey

1 Put the duck legs skin-side down in a deep pan and pour over the soy sauce and enough water to cover. Add the ginger, garlic, star anise and the cinnamon stick, cover with a lid and bring to the boil. Reduce the heat to a gentle simmer and cook for 30 mins.

2 Turn the duck legs over and continue poaching for 1 hr or until tender. Remove from the heat and set aside to cool, then remove from the cooking liquor.

3 Meanwhile, bring a pan of water to the boil, cook the broccoli for 2 mins then rinse in cold water and set aside. Put the kale in a large bowl, cover with boiling water and leave for 1 min. Drain and rinse under cold water, then set aside.

4 Heat the air fryer to 180°C/350°F. Cook the duck, skin side up, on an air fryer liner for 10 mins, then increase the heat to 200°C/400°F and cook for 3 mins until crisp. Shred the duck while it is still hot. Combine the dressing ingredients until smooth, then toss with the kale, broccoli, duck and seeds. It will keep, dressed, for 4 hrs.

Roasted Heritage Carrots and Parsnips with Orange and Za'atar

You can easily upgrade this to a veggie main dish by adding chickpeas and serving with couscous. You may need to cook two batches, but simply reheat the first by air frying for a min or two

Serves 4 * Ready in 20 minutes

* 500g (1lb 1oz) medium heritage carrots, cleaned and halved lengthways
* 300g (10½oz) parsnips, cleaned and halved lengthways
* 1 orange, sliced
* 2tsp cumin seeds
* 1tbsp za'atar
* ¼tsp crushed chillies
* 4 garlic cloves
* 3tbsp olive oil
* 1½tbsp honey
* 5tbsp Greek yoghurt
* 1tbsp tahini

1 Put the carrots and parsnips in a bowl. Add the orange slices, cumin seeds, za'atar, chillies and garlic and season with salt, then toss thoroughly with the olive oil and honey.

2 Heat the air fryer to 180°C/350°F. Roast for 12 mins, shaking halfway through, until the vegetables are tender and golden.

3 Combine the yoghurt and tahini in a small bowl. Season lightly with salt and add a little crushed chilli, if you like. Serve alongside the roasted carrots and parsnips.

Chestnut, Mushroom and Cider Pie

These cute, creamy pies make a lovely veggie supper. If making the filling ahead, reheat it before air frying, or the pastry will be cooked through but the filling not piping hot

Serves 2 • Ready in 50 minutes

- 1tbsp olive oil
- 1 red onion, thickly sliced
- 25g (1oz) dried porcini mushrooms
- 125g (4½oz) button mushrooms
- 125g (4½oz) chestnut mushrooms, sliced
- 225g (8oz) chestnuts, sliced
- 2tbsp fresh thyme leaves
- 300ml (10fl oz) dry cider
- 4tbsp double cream
- 150g (5oz) all-butter puff pastry
- 1 egg yolk

You will need:
2 individual pie dishes

1 Heat the oil in a large sauté pan and cook the onion until just soft. Meanwhile, cover the porcini with hot water and leave to soak for 15 mins. Add the button and chestnut mushrooms to the onion and sauté on a high heat for a few mins. Drain the porcini, reserving the liquid, and add them to the rest of the mushrooms. Add the chestnuts and thyme and mix together. Season well.

2 Add the cider and 150ml (5fl oz) soaking liquid from the porcini, bring to the boil then simmer gently for 15 mins. Add the cream; remove from the heat to cool. This filling will keep for 2 days in the fridge.
3 When the filling is cool, divide the mix between 2 dishes. Cut out 2 circles of pastry, each 1cm (½in) larger than the dish. Brush the outer edge with egg yolk and place the pastry on it. Glaze the top with the egg yolk, refrigerate for 5 mins.
4 Heat the air fryer to 190°C/375°F. Cook for 15 mins, or until browned and bubbling.

Chaat Style Roast Potatoes

Give leftover roasties a new lease of life with this Indian-inspired potato snack

Serves 6 • Ready in 30 minutes

* 1-2tbsp sunflower oil
* 1tbsp chaat masala, or garam masala
* ½tsp curry powder
* ¼tsp fennel seeds, crushed
* 500g (1lb 1oz) leftover roast potatoes and parsnips

FOR THE MINT SAUCE:
* Small bunch fresh mint leaves, chopped
* Small bunch fresh coriander leaves, chopped
* 2tsp mint sauce
* Juice 1 lemon
* 2tsp olive oil

FOR THE TOPPINGS:
* 125g (4oz) natural yoghurt
* 2tbsp pomegranate seeds
* 1 fresh green chilli, chopped
* 1tsp tamarind chutney, mixed with a dash of water to form a drizzle, or use pomegranate molasses
* 2tbsp leftover crisps or Bombay mix, crushed

1 Combine the oil with the chaat masala, curry powder and fennel seeds, drizzle over the potatoes and parsnips, and toss to coat. Heat the air fryer to 180°C/350°F. Bake the mixture for 12 mins, shaking halfway through.
2 Meanwhile, mix together the ingredients for the mint sauce.
3 Put the potatoes and parsnips in a serving dish, and drizzle over the yoghurt, mint sauce, pomegranate seeds, chilli and tamarind chutney. Top with crisps or Bombay mix.

Squash Fondue

A winter-warming lunch for four which will transport you straight to snowy mountains. Just ensure the squash are the correct size to fit together into your air fryer

Serves 4 * Ready in 50 minutes

* 4 winter squash, tops sliced off
* 60g (2½oz) soft salted butter
* A handful of sage leaves
* Oil spray
* 350ml (12fl oz) dry white wine
* 150ml (5fl oz) milk
* 400g (14oz) Gruyère, or hard cheese, grated
* 2tbsp plain flour
* Crusty bread, to serve

1 Scrape the seeds out of the squash (reserving any shiny, plump seeds). Rub the insides with most of the butter.
2 Pop a sage leaf or 2 into each squash and season. Heat the air fryer to 180°C/350°F. Put the squash on an air fryer liner, together with the lids, spray with oil and bake for 20 mins or until tender.
3 Pour the wine into a saucepan and bring to the boil for a few secs, then reduce to a simmer. Pour the milk into another pan and gently warm through. Toss 350g (12oz) of cheese with the flour.
4 Add the flour-coated cheese to the wine, a handful at a time, stirring between each addition until melted. Gradually whisk in the milk, then season.
5 Divide this mixture between the squash.
6 Top with the remaining Gruyère and return to the air fryer for 15 mins, until golden. Rub the remaining butter over the rest of the sage leaves along with any seeds. Quickly pan-fry for a few mins. Serve with bread for dipping.

Baked Camembert with Garlic and White Wine

Baking a whole cheese is a speedy way to serve a fondue. Ensure your Camembert is ripe and at room temperature

Serves 2 • Ready in 20 minutes

- 1 small (about 250g/9oz) Camembert in a wooden box
- 1 garlic clove, sliced
- A handful of thyme sprigs
- A splash of white wine
- Warm, crusty bread and chicory leaves, to dip

1 Unwrap the cheese, discarding any paper or plastic wrapping but keeping the box and lid. Carefully slice off just the top rind, then make shallow cuts into the surface of the cheese and insert slices of garlic and tiny sprigs of thyme. Return the cheese to its box, cut-side up. Heat the air fryer to 180°C/350°F.

2. Douse with a splash of white wine and bake, uncovered, for 15 mins until the cheese is molten. Serve with hunks of warm bread and a pile of crisp chicory leaves for dipping.

Bubble and Squeak

The ultimate Boxing Day brunch dish with no frying required. Serve with your sausages, bacon or a soft-poached egg

Serves 4 · **Ready in 30 minutes**

- 750g (1lb 10oz) leftover roast or mashed potatoes
- A little milk, cream or crème fraîche, optional
- 50g (2oz) butter
- 1 large onion, chopped
- 400g (14oz) leftover green vegetables, roughly chopped
- 3tbsp capers
- Oil spray

1 If using roast potatoes, mash roughly in a large bowl, adding a couple of tablespoons of milk, cream or crème fraîche if they're a little dry.

2 Melt half the butter in a frying pan and gently cook the onion for 10 mins until soft. In a large bowl, mix together the potato, onion, vegetables and capers. Season well.

3 Heat the air fryer to 200°C/400°F. Shape the mixture into 8 patties, spray with oil and cook on a silicone mat for 10 mins, then flip and cook for 6 mins.

Cook's tip
If you don't have any leftover greens, use any type of cabbage, lightly steaming it first.